Ponderosa

PONDEROSA
Big Pine of the Southwest

SYLVESTER ALLRED

THE UNIVERSITY OF
ARIZONA PRESS

TUCSON

The University of Arizona Press
www.uapress.arizona.edu

Printed in the United States of America
20 19 18 17 16 15   6 5 4 3 2 1

ISBN-(paper)13: 978-0-8165-3143-1

Cover designed by Leigh McDonald
Cover photo by Sylvester Allred

All photographs are by the author unless otherwise noted.

Publication of this book was made possible in part by funding from
The Arboretum at Flagstaff, the Center of Southwest Studies at Fort
Lewis College, the Department of Biological Sciences at Northern
Arizona University, Grand Canyon Wildlands Council, the Landscape
Conservation Initiative at Northern Arizona University, and The
Southwest Center at the University of Arizona.

Library of Congress Cataloging-in-Publication Data
Allred, Sylvester, 1946– author.
    Ponderosa : big pine of the Southwest / Sylvester Allred.
        pages cm
    Includes bibliographical references and index.
    ISBN 978-0-8165-3143-1 (pbk. : alk. paper)
    1. Ponderosa pine—Southwest, New. 2. Forest ecology—Southwest,
New. I. Title.
    QK494.5.P66A52 2015
    577.30979—dc23
                                                    2014030798

∞ This paper meets the requirements of ANSI/NISO Z39.48–1992
(Permanence of Paper).

In memory of my parents,
Mildred Ella Skinner Allred and
William Sylvester Allred, and
my father-in-law, James W. Nelson

Contents

Illustrations

Figures

Plates

Preface

In 1911 Albert W. Palmer published accounts of some Sierra Club summer outings in *The Mountain Trail and Its Message*. Mr. Palmer's description of an encounter with John Muir, one of my heroes, is an ideal guide for reading and using this book:

> There are always some people in the mountains who are known as "hikers." They rush over the trail at high speed and take great delight in being the first to reach camp and in covering the greatest number of miles in the least possible time. They measure the trail in terms of speed and distance.
>
> One day as I was resting in the shade Mr. Muir overtook me on the trail and began to chat in that friendly way in which he delights to talk with everyone he meets. I said to him: "Mr. Muir, someone told me you did not approve of the word 'hike.' Is that so?" His blue eyes flashed, and with his Scotch accent he replied: "I don't like either the word or the thing. People ought to saunter in the mountains—not hike!"
>
> Do you know the origin of that word "saunter"? It's a beautiful word. Away back in the Middle Ages people used to go on pilgrimages to the Holy Land, and when people in the villages through which they passed asked where they were going, they would reply, "A la sainte terre." "To the Holy Land." And so they became known as sainte-terre-ers or saunterers. Now these mountains are our Holy Land, and we ought to saunter through them reverently, not "hike" through them.
>
> John Muir lived up to his doctrine. He was usually the last man to reach camp. He never hurried. He stopped to get acquainted with individual trees along the way. He would hail people passing by and make them get down on hands and knees if necessary to see the beauty of some little bed of almost microscopic flowers. Usually he appeared at camp with some new flowers in his hat and a little piece of fir bough in his buttonhole.

As you saunter through the ponderosas making new discoveries and memories, follow John Muir's advice. Stop often, look around, feel the furrowed bark of the blackjacks and smell

between the deep furrows of yellowbellies. Touch the pine needles, both the green ones on the branches and the yellow-brown
ones underfoot. Pick up a prickly brown pinecone and marvel
at its intricate architecture. Allow your eyes to find unnamed
colors that do not appear in those boxes full of wax sticks with
artificial names.

    Let your saunter begin.

Acknowledgments

Authoring a book requires numerous individuals who provide support in many ways, from the initial idea to the final copyediting. The following are among those who assisted me.

Donna Nelson, my wife, spent many hours going through each page of every new draft of this book—and there were many. She was always ready with wonderful ideas, creative suggestions, ever-flowing encouragement, and editing advice.

Meribeth Watwood, chair of the Department of Biological Sciences at Northern Arizona University, contributed generous departmental backing for this endeavor.

John Westerlund planted the seed that grew into this book.

Six reviewers gave their comments and recommendations.

Numerous individuals granted permission for the use of their artwork and photographs. Each is acknowledged in the caption.

Copyediting of the final manuscript was expertly done by Mindy Conner.

Numerous individuals at the University of Arizona Press from the planning, marketing, production, and distribution departments provided their expertise. I began the conversation about this book with Allyson Carter, the press's editor-in-chief, in the late fall of 2008. Allyson was receptive from the beginning and always offered me encouragement. I am grateful.

Author's Note

The trees are large and noble in aspect and stand widely apart, except in the highest part of the plateau where spruces predominate. Instead of dense thickets where we are shut in by impenetrable foliage, we can look far beyond and see the tree trunks vanishing away like an infinite colonnade. The ground is unobstructed and inviting. There is a constant succession of parks and glades, dream avenues of grass and flowers winding between sylvan walls, or spreading out in broad open meadows. From June until September there is a display of wildflowers which is quite beyond description.

—CLARENCE DUTTON, *PHYSICAL GEOLOGY OF THE GRAND CANYON DISTRICT* (1887)

In midsummer of 1889 C. Hart Merriam traveled to the San Francisco Peaks in northern Arizona Territory to study biotic communities with respect to their elevation and latitude. The San Francisco Peaks, sacred to thirteen Native American tribes, were named in honor of Saint Francis of Assisi in the early seventeenth century by members of a Franciscan mission at the Hopi village of Oraibi. Rising 12,633 feet to the top of Humphreys Peak, these mountains offered an excellent location for Merriam to compare the dominant vegetation growing at specific elevations, which he referred to as life zones. Merriam's Transition zone, situated between 5,000 and 7,000 feet, contained ponderosa pine trees, and thus the ponderosa pine became the indicator plant for that life zone. Pinyon-juniper forests growing below 5,000 feet and aspen-spruce-fir forests growing above 7,000 feet act as the boundaries of the Transition zone.

In a description of the region he published in 1890, Merriam emphasized the parklike quality of the ponderosa pine forest:

The lofty pine forest of the San Francisco Mountain Plateau has been famous since the days of the early explorers, Sitgreaves, Kennerly, and Ives, who passed through it on their journeys across the continent. It is a noteworthy forest, not alone on account of the size and beauty of the single species of tree of which it is composed (*Pinus ponderosa*), but also because of its openness, freedom from undergrowth, and its grassy carpet—for the porous lava soil supports a sparse growth of bunch-grass which is high enough after the rainy season sets in to conceal the rocky surface, and, at a little distance, to present the appearance of a meadow. *

Three varieties of ponderosa pines grow in North America. This book is about the natural history of the ponderosa pine (variety scoplorum, commonly known as the Rocky Mountain ponderosa pine) that lives in the southwestern United States. Even though this book is written with emphasis on ponderosas of the Southwest, it can be used as a general reference for the ponderosas in other areas of the species's range. The extensive list of references at the end of this book, divided into twenty-one alphabetized categories, provides more information.

---

* C. H. Merriam and L. Stejneger, *Results of a Biological Survey of the San Francisco Mountain Region and the Desert of the Little Colorado, Arizona,* North American Fauna 3 (Washington, DC: U.S. Department of Agriculture, Division of Ornithology and Mammalia, 1890).

Plate 1. Ponderosa pine trees.

Ponderosa

Figure 1. San Francisco Peaks, Arizona, and ponderosa pine forest, 1890. (From C. H. Merriam and L. Stejneger. 1890. *Results of a Biological Survey of the San Francisco Mountain Region and the Desert of the Little Colorado, Arizona.* North American Fauna 3. U.S. Department of Agriculture, Division of Ornithology and Mammalia, Washington, DC.)

Introduction

I spent most of my academic and research career in Flagstaff, Arizona, the site of the largest contiguous ponderosa pine forest in the world. For twenty-seven years I studied tassel-eared squirrels, unique little creatures that live only in ponderosa pine forests. During the thousands of hours I spent amid these magnificent trees I observed the intricacies of the life of the ponderosa pine forest. Through this book I will share my experiences, thoughts, and observations with you.

In the course of our saunter through the ponderosa forests we will see healthy forests and forests that are weakened and struggling. We will visit forests that have been burned, some by careless humans and some by fires started by lightning. We will look for evidence of insects and spiders in the bark. We will learn where to smell butterscotch and vanilla and other flavors. We will watch squirrels dig for false truffles and hide pinecones for future use. We may see where male deer and elk rubbed their antlers on saplings to remove the velvet during the rutting season. We will hear the noisy squawks of the beautiful blue Steller's jay. We will see tiny seedlings popping through the ground and ancient trees with golden-reddish bark. We will see nature's sculptures—the standing snags that are home to myriad insects, birds, and bats. After a snowstorm we will see who has been out and about as we look for tracks, fur, feathers, and bloodstains, evidence of both predator and prey. On a saunter in the spring we will see lovely penstemons with their assorted bright and pastel-colored petals resembling open mouths with tongues thrust forward, a plethora of yellow composite flowers with their petals arranged in a windmill pattern, and cerulean lupines with their bee landing platforms and green pods filled with tiny black seeds. We will see the purple vetches and the louse-worts, so named because many centuries ago it was thought that these plants prevented lice infestations. In open sunlit meadows we will see biennial mullein plants with tall, candelabra-shaped stalks loaded with yellow flowers that produce tiny black seeds smaller than the period at the end of this sentence. When the mullein dies in the fall the brown stalks remain standing, and the touch of a deer or elk or human hand on the dried stalk will catapult thousands of seeds outward. This explains why mullein plants are often found in clumps. In the summer and fall we may see strange reddish-brown pinedrops beneath the towering ponderosas.

Tassel-Eared Squirrels—Important Members of the Ponderosa Pine Forests

Four subspecies of tassel-eared squirrels live in the ponderosa forests of the Southwest. The ponderosas provide the squirrels with foods, nest sites, and nest-building materials. Foods include the inner bark of pine twigs, pollen cones, and seeds from the pinecones. The squirrels also eat false truffles—fungi that live in association with ponderosa pine roots. The fungi increase the tree's ability to absorb water and nutrients, and the tree provides sugars for the fungi. The squirrels use their keen sense of smell to locate the truffles. As the squirrels scurry through the forests they disperse the spores of the fungi in their fecal pellets. The spores enter the soil and inoculate other pine roots, benefitting the entire forest. The ponderosa pine, the tassel-eared squirrel, and the false truffles constitute a unique triad, each dependent on the others for survival.

An Example of Natural Selection

Before a squirrel begins to feed on the inner bark of a ponderosa pine, it tastes a sample. Some trees have distasteful chemicals that protect them from further nibbling; trees that are not chemically defended become "feed trees." The chemicals produced by "nonfeed" trees are an adaptation against herbivory (eating plant materials) and are a heritable characteristic. Natural selection, the driving force behind evolution, acts on such genetically determined variations. Sometimes the variations are beneficial, sometimes they are neutral, and sometimes they are lethal. Natural selection tends to keep beneficial and neutral variations within the gene pool of the species.

Plate 2. Tassel-eared squirrel. The squirrels depend on ponderosa pine forests for food and shelter. (Photograph by Steve Mull. Used with permission.)

In the fall abundant mushrooms raise their colorful caps above the forest floor litter, each cap filled with millions of spores. Other fungi live their entire lives hidden beneath the soil, but we may see evidence of their presence in the form of "digs" of tassel-eared squirrels seeking this food source.

While we saunter we will talk about the challenges of managing the forests in a way that satisfies the needs both of those seeking recreation and respite and of those who utilize the forests commercially for timber harvesting and cattle grazing. We will talk about the past history of the majestic ponderosas and look toward the future of the ponderosa pine forest ecosystem in the face of climate change and human encroachment.

If you have ponderosa pines in your backyard and you want to know what makes every surface in your house yellow in late spring, or why the big cones in your yard have prickles, this book is written for you. If you are an outdoor enthusiast who enjoys a stroll through the forest, this book is written for you. If you want to take a day hike, camp, or backpack in a ponderosa pine forest in any of the public parks or forests in the southwestern United States, this book is written for you. For the interpretive park ranger or the student of biology, ecology, environment science, or forestry—or for any other student of our Earth wishing to know more—this book offers fun facts and a list of references sufficient to guide you to every aspect of the vast research that has been published since the first mention of the ponderosa in the scientific literature two hundred years ago.

You can spend an hour, an afternoon, or a lifetime exploring a ponderosa pine forest. This book can be your guide.

Where Are the Ponderosa Pine Forests?

The range of the ponderosa pine extends from British Columbia, Canada, to the mountain ranges of northern Mexico and includes almost one-third of the states in the United States. Ponderosa pine forests are found at elevations ranging from sea level to ten thousand feet within that range and cover nearly twenty-seven million acres in the United States. The forests in the southwestern United States occur between five thousand and eight thousand feet. Ponderosa pine forests can be found in national parks and forests; on public lands administered by the Bureau of Land Management; and on state trust lands, forests, and parks in the southwestern United States.

I have done most of my sauntering in ponderosa pine forests across the street and up the hill from my house; on the forested land on the mesa owned by Lowell Observatory, where Pluto was discovered in 1930; and on the beautiful San Francisco Peaks, which I saw every day from my home in Flagstaff.*

---

* Flagstaff was first referred to as "Flag Staff" in 1876 when a group of settlers traveling west to California stripped a tall ponderosa of its branches and raised the U.S. flag with its thirty-seven stars to the top of the tree to celebrate the Centennial on July 4. You can learn more of this fascinating story in works by Richard and Sherry Mangum, who have written many hiking and guide books about Flagstaff and surrounding areas.

Plate 3. San Francisco Peaks near Flagstaff, Arizona. Humphreys Peak, the highest elevation in Arizona, rises to an elevation of 12,633 feet.

Pinus ponderosa

SCALE 1: 15000000

100 0 100 200 300 400 500 MILES

100 0 100 200 300 400 500 KILOMETERS

≋USGS
science for a changing world

Figure 2. The distribution of ponderosa pine forests in North America and Mexico. (From U.S. Geological Survey, http://gec.cr.usgs.gov/ data/little/pinupond.pdf.)

Pinus ponderosa, Cone-Bearers, and Naked Seeds

During late July 1776, the Dominguez-Escalante expedition departed Santa Fe on a journey through the area that is now Colorado, Utah, and Arizona; they returned to Santa Fe in January 1777. Early in the course of the expedition the group passed through forests in northern New Mexico and southern Utah. The trees are not named or described in the expedition journals, but translated journal entries pinpoint their locations. Those notes and the ages of present-day trees make it almost certain that the forests the expedition traversed contained ponderosa pines.

Meriwether Lewis and William Clark called the massive pine trees they saw in 1805 "long-leaf pines" in their expedition's journals. Twenty-one years later a young Scottish botanist, David Douglas, gave the trees their scientific name, *Pinus ponderosa* (ponderous pine), while exploring the Pacific Northwest. Douglas (for whom the Douglas-fir is named) died in 1834 in Hawaii at the young age of thirty-five after falling into a pit used to trap wild cattle. His untimely gory death was never fully explained. "Ponderosa" became the official common name in 1932, replacing other common names such as big pine, black pine, bull pine, western yellow pine, and yellow pine. The official abbreviation of "ponderosa pine" is PIPO, derived by combining the first two letters of the genus (*Pinus*) and the first two letters of the species (*ponderosa*). Scientists and foresters use the abbreviation in their reports, papers, and journal articles.

Ponderosa pines belong to the group of plants called gymnosperms—from the Greek word meaning "naked seed." The seeds are naked (i.e., not enclosed in fruits) and are found on

Plate 4. Open female ponderosa pinecone showing bracts. Each bract has a short prickle at its end. The winged, BB-size seeds form in the two depressions at the base of each bract.

the bracts of the cones. All the trees we recognize as conifers, or cone-bearers, are gymnosperms. Most conifers are evergreen (there are exceptions to every rule; e.g., larches and bald cypresses), and their slender, pointed leaves are called needles. Evergreen trees retain their needles year-round while most deciduous trees lose their leaves during the fall.

In contrast to the gymnosperms, the seeds of flowering plants, called angiosperms (e.g., tulips and roses and maples and oaks), are enclosed by fruit tissue. Think about where you find the seeds of the fruit of a pea, an apple, and an avocado: they are enclosed.

The first gymnosperms made their appearance on Earth about 375 million years ago during the Devonian geological time

Eon	*Era*	*Period*	*Millions of Years Ago*
Phanerozoic	Cenozoic	Quaternary	
		Tertiary	1.6
	Mesozoic	Cretaceous	66
		Jurassic	138
		Triassic	205
	Paleozoic	Permian	240
		Pennsylvanian	290
		Mississippian	330
		Devonian	360
		Silurian	410
		Ordovician	435
		Cambrian	500
Proterozoic	Late Proterozoic Middle Proterozoic Early Proterozoic		570
Archean	Late Archean Middle Archean Early Archean		2,500
	Pre-Archean		3,800?

NOTES: Angiosperms (flowering plants) appeared 140 million years ago (MYA). Gymnosperms appeared 375 MYA.
SOURCE: http://pubs.usgs.gov/gip/fossils/numeric.html

Figure 3. Geological time scale. (From U.S. Geological Survey, http://pubs.usgs.gov/gip/fossils/numeric.html.)

period. Some 235 million years would pass before the first angio-sperms developed! The earliest fossilized ponderosas, found in Nevada, are 600,000 years old.

Yellowbellies, Blackjacks, and Spiral Growth

Just as we can tell at a glance whether a person is a teenager or someone who has enjoyed many years, we can tell at a glance the approximate age of a ponderosa pine. Blackjacks are the youngsters of the ponderosas and are so called because of their dark bark, which may be gray, dark brown, or black. When ponderosas reach the age of about one hundred they develop a distinctive deep orange to rust-red color and are then referred

Plate 5. Yellowbellies and blackjacks. Note their distinctive bark colors.

to as yellowbellies. Field research has shown that blackjacks start to transition to yellowbellies when they approach 18 to 22 inches diameter at breast height. Some of the oldest trees may reach heights of 230 feet and may exceed 6 feet in diameter.

The shape of a tree gives us information about its age as well. The crown of younger trees (the area with all the needles) tapers upward into a point resembling a pyramid. As the trees mature, their crowns become more rounded; the oldest trees have flattened crowns. The oldest known ponderosa is 935 years old (as of 2014) and is found in Utah. Some of the trees in the forests where I saunter are 500–600 years old!

The bark of a ponderosa is divided into plates, referred to as bark plates; as yellowbellies become very large, deep furrows develop between the plates. In *The Mountains of California* (1894), John Muir described the bark plates of older ponderosa pine trees as "four or five feet in length by eighteen inches in width, with a thickness of three to four inches." The furrows between the plates are home to myriad insects and spiders. Watch the nuthatches moving stealthily upside down on the tree, probing for food. Look for their relatives, the tiny brown creepers, sauntering sideways along the bark, head-up, looking for invertebrate morsels hiding within the cracks.

Yellowbellies produce chemicals in their bark that may smell like vanilla, butterscotch, caramel, chocolate, or pineapple, depending on your imagination. You can detect the fragrance by sniffing between bark plates. But look first! Remember: insects and spiders live in these furrows, too.

A common method of estimating the age of ponderosas involves taking a sample core of the trunk at "breast height" (bh), which foresters define to be 4.5 feet above the ground (not the chest height of the person taking the measurement!). The tree's diameter is measured at bh, and the resulting measurement is referred to as the diameter (d) at breast height, or dbh. In a study conducted in a ponderosa pine forest in northern Arizona in 1964, Charles Minor determined that "the time required for the 91 trees studied to reach breast height (4.5 feet) averaged 14.3 years and ranged from 6 to 29 years." However, even though the bh method of aging is the standard measurement used by foresters, it does underestimate the actual age of the tree.

To take a core, a tool called an increment borer is twisted into the center of the tree at bh, and a core about the width and shape of a soda straw is removed. The growth rings in the core, which appear as separate layers, are counted and examined with

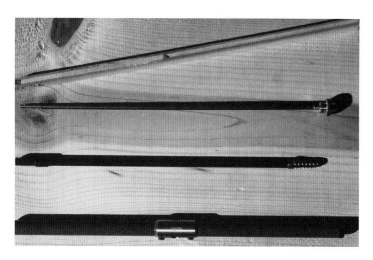

Plate 6. Tree-coring tool and a tree core. This tool is used to remove a core of a living tree to determine its approximate age.

magnification. The width of the individual growth rings can be indicative of past climates—dry or wet, cold or hot. The coring process does not harm the tree. The hole made by the borer fills in with resin that seals the opening and protects the tree from infections.

Each year a tree produces a growth ring that is divided into two parts: the light springwood, or early-wood ring; and the dark summerwood, or later-wood ring. The springwood is lighter in color because there is usually more moisture available during the spring, enabling a flush of new growth; the cell walls of the xylem cells in springwood are relatively thin with wider openings. The summerwood is darker because there is less moisture available for growth, and the xylem cells walls are thicker, making the ring look darker. The dark rings are easier to count, but some foresters count all the rings—light and dark—and divide by two to determine the approximate age of the tree. Approximate, because in years of low moisture the rings formed are narrow and faint and may be difficult to distinguish without magnification.

Tree rings become smaller as the tree grows larger, regardless of the weather conditions. Competition with other trees can also affect tree ring size. Trees that grow in the open in full sun, unblocked by the canopies of nearby trees, tend to have larger growth rings.

Plate 7. Growth rings. When examining a tree stump, count just the dark or light rings or count all the rings and divide by two to reach an approximate age for the tree.

A. E. Douglass and Dendrochronology

Andrew Ellicott Douglass (1867–1962), an astronomer, founded the field of dendrochronology in 1894 while working with Percival Lowell at Lowell Observatory in Flagstaff, Arizona. After leaving Lowell he went to the University of Arizona, where he became the first director of the Laboratory of Tree-Ring Research. During his career at the university he was involved in southwestern archaeological investigations examining and establishing dates of buildings and ruins found at Aztec, Pueblo Bonito, Mesa Verde, and Canyon de Chelly. By examining beams from those structures he was able to correlate ages of tree rings of living trees with the rings found in the beams, a technique he called "cross-dating."

In 1920 Douglass published a paper in the journal *Ecology* in which he presented a relationship between tree growth and climate, as opposed to just tree growth and rainfall patterns. The editor attached a note to the end of Douglass's paper, stating, "Dr. Douglass' development of the idea . . . represents a marked step forward in this important line of research."

Tree-ring research has scientific applications in understanding the past activities of glaciers, hurricanes, tidal waves, volcanoes, and fires. The Laboratory of Tree-Ring Research, established in 1937, is recognized as one of the best tree-ring research sites in the world. By examining rings of trees from different areas that lived during the same time periods, scientists can compare climatic regimes (especially moisture) across wide regions. This information can be used to predict future climatic trends in a geographical area. For more on the subject, visit the lab's website, http://ltrr.arizona.edu.

The dating and study of growth rings is called dendrochronology. Dendrochronological studies help to establish what the climate was at the time a particular ring or series of rings was formed. As you saunter through the forest, look for a stump where you can see and count the growth rings. Note that some are widely spaced and some are narrow. Can you interpret this observation to determine what the climate was at the time the rings were formed?

While it can certainly be said that a yellowbelly ponderosa is old, its exact age is just a guess without the tree ring calculation. Trees that grow in nutrient-rich soils, in moist soils, or in sites not shaded by other trees will be larger at the same age than trees growing in more adverse conditions. Even the direction of the slope may affect the growth because north-facing slopes tend to retain more moisture than south-facing slopes.

Plate 8. Yellowbelly with a forked trunk in the Kaibab National Forest near Jacob Lake, Arizona. The ponderosas in the Kaibab National Forest and along the North Rim of the Grand Canyon are among the oldest in Arizona.

Plate 9. Shapes of ponderosas showing the tree's age and growth pattern. The tree in the foreground has a pyramidal shape indicative of further upward growth; the trees in the background have flattened tops indicative of maturing trees.

The roots of ponderosas begin growing in early spring. In late spring leaf buds open, pollen cones appear, and the diameter of the tree begins to increase. Active growth, which is contingent on soil moisture, temperature, and day length, continues until the seeds mature in mid-fall, although growth can be retarded or accelerated by increases or decreases in those three environmental components. During the winter photosynthesis can continue at low rates if soil temperatures are warm enough for the tree to take up water and there is adequate sunlight, but there is no active growth of stems or needles.

Dendromorphometry is the science of measuring living trees using a mathematical model that incorporates numerous tree dimensions such as height, girth, and crown spread. It is a useful forest management tool for foresters.

Have you noticed that some ponderosa pines (and other types of trees as well) have a spiral growth pattern? This pattern is best seen in trees that have been struck by lightning and in decaying trees with missing bark. When lightning enters the tree at the top, it spirals toward the ground along this growth pattern, which resembles a barber pole. Ponderosas are great lightning rods!

Plate 10. Lightning scar showing the tree's spiral growth pattern.

Pay close attention as you saunter along mountainous ridges and rock outcrops and you will see quite a few lightning-struck trees, many still alive.

It may be that the spiral growth pattern dissipates some of the lightning's energy in the course of its coiling path to the ground, possibly allowing the tree to survive the strike. There is more water (a good electrical conductor) in the xylem and sapwood nearer to the bark, so the lightning is conducted downward through this part of the tree, blowing off the tree's bark as it goes. It seems feasible that if the bark explodes outward, the energy of the lightning strike will be dispersed away from the center of the tree. Based on my hundreds of observations, lightning does destroy some trees, literally blowing them apart, but that seems to be the exception rather than the rule.

Spiral growth appears to be more prevalent in areas where trees are exposed to high winds, such as ridgelines. Spiral growth strengthens the tree in the same way that the spiraling of steel cables used on suspension bridges adds strength to those structures. Natural selection has clearly favored this growth pattern over a straight-grained pattern.

Reasons other than strengthening have been proposed to explain spiral growth in trees. Some theories relate to its effect on nutrient and water distribution within the tree. Others propose that the Earth's rotation, magnetic fields, and solar exposure are somehow involved. Spiraling is common in the natural world; think of seashells, the tooth of the narwhal, the horns of bighorn sheep, the inner ear, tornados, hurricanes, and galaxies.

One House, Winged Seeds, and Golden Pollen

Ponderosa pines are monoecious; that is, each tree produces both male and female cones. The term "monoecious" derives from a Greek word meaning "one house." The female cones begin forming in late spring as tiny conelets; they can occur either singly or in clusters of up to five as they develop alongside the leaf buds. These conelets contain the eggs that will be fertilized when the male pinecones release their sperm-containing pollen in late May–early June of year one. Seed fall occurs in September–October of the following year (year two). This reproductive

Plate 11. Young green ponderosa pine conelet cluster at the tip of a branch.

Plate 12. Slightly older purple ponderosa pine conelet cluster at the tip of a branch. This color change occurs after a few weeks to several months of development.

pattern is very different from that of other conifers, in which seeds mature and fall in the same season in which pollination occurs. The deep purple color of the female conelets will change to light green during the two-year period required for the development and maturation of the cones and seeds. At maturity the female cones are bright green and very conspicuous in clusters near the end of a branch.

Female cones are composed of a woody core with attached woody cone bracts. The bracts are arranged around the central core in a spiral from the bottom of the cone to its apex and follow the Fibonacci sequence. Each bract holds two seeds. Even though the tightly closed green cones protect the developing

Plate 13. Mature female ponderosa pinecones. Note the sharp prickle at the end of each bract. The cones contain copious resins and average sixty seeds per cone.

Plate 14. Longitudinal section of an opened female ponderosa pinecone showing the woody structures.

seeds with copious resin, and each bract has a tiny sharp prickle to defend it, squirrels and birds such as crossbills can open the cones and eat the seeds.

Two winged seeds form at the base on the inside surface of each bract of the female cone. Locate an opened cone in the litter layer and carefully pull back a bract to find the depressions where the seeds formed. Each seed is about one-fourth to one-half inch long, including the wing, and each cone contains between thirty and eighty seeds. The weight of ponderosa pine seeds is highly variable; there may be between seven thousand and twenty-three thousand seeds in a pound. Birds, squirrels, and other rodents eat ponderosa pine seeds, and Native Americans used them for food. Ponderosa seeds are wind dispersed, unlike the seeds of some other pines. Pinyon pine seeds, for example, are dispersed by birds—Clark's nutcrackers and pinyon jays.

Female Pinecones and Their Relationship to the Fibonacci Series

Pick up a female pinecone from the litter layer. Turn it so that the larger end is facing you. Note the growth pattern of the cone bracts. They are arranged in a spiral that follows the Fibonacci sequence of numbers: 0, 1, 1, 2, 3, 5, 8, 13, 21 . . . The next number in the sequence is determined by adding the previous two together; in this example the next number is 34. Can you determine the next number after that? Leonardo Fibonacci di Pisa, an Italian mathematician, discovered this mathematical phenomenon during the 1100s. The Fibonacci sequence occurs elsewhere in nature, too—for example, in seashells, artichokes, and sunflower seed heads.

Plate 15. Bottom end of an opened female ponderosa pine cone demonstrating the Fibonacci series.

Plate 16. Male ponderosa pinecones. The golden yellow cones release their pollen into the air, creating huge clouds of yellow dust in ponderosa pine forests during May and June.

The small yellow-brown male cones are much less substantial than the sturdy female cones. They appear in late spring, then turn golden and release their pollen between May and June, creating large yellow clouds throughout the forest. In urban settings the pollen covers every surface with a fine yellow powder. The male cones, each about an inch long, occur in dense clusters around the bud tip. After pollen release the work of the male cones is done; they dry out, turn brown, and fall to the ground, where they quickly break up in the litter layer. Pine pollen is rich in nutrients and calories, and tassel-eared squirrels eat the male pinecones before the pollen is released. Pollen dusts their faces with gold during the short pollen season and turns their fecal pellets gold as well.

Tiny Seedlings

When sauntering through the forest, be sure to look down at the nursery, the tiny green seedlings pushing up through the brown needles of the litter layer. These are best seen in late summer after the rains. The first set of needles looks like small, green, twisted fingers reaching upward. For a short time these needles still have the seed coat attached, which appears as a little brown ball. Some of these seedlings owe their existence to a small rodent or bird that cached a single seed at the right depth and never came back to eat it. Competition for space, nutrients, water, and sunlight is severe, and many seedlings die the first year. Those that do survive face new tests such as being nibbled by insects, birds, and mammals, including elk, deer, rabbits, and squirrels and other small rodents. Fungal infections and frost heave during heavy freezes also take a toll on seedlings.

The American naturalist Enos Mills marveled that in the face of these difficulties "trees should live to become the oldest of living things. Fastened in one place, their struggle is incessant and severe. From the moment a baby tree is born—from the instant it casts its tiny shadow upon the ground—until death, it is in danger from insects and animals. It cannot move to avoid danger. It cannot run away to escape enemies. Fixed in one spot, almost helpless, it must endure flood and drought, fire and storm, insects and earthquakes, or die." *

---

* Enos Mills, *The Story of the Thousand-Year Pine* (1914)

Plate 17. Ponderosa pine seedlings.

On occasion you may see a group of seedlings so thickly packed together in little bunches that their needles resemble many newly sprouted grass blades. This can occur when a squirrel buries an entire green unopened cone. When an abundant cone crop (a natural occurrence every seven or eight years) is coupled with ample precipitation, many seeds will germinate and many seedlings will survive. If the seedlings are not thinned by fire or by humans, they will produce extremely dense stands of stunted trees known as dog-hair thickets. Such clusters can

Plate 18. Dog-hair thicket of ponderosa pine trees in the foreground with yellowbellies in the background. These spindly trees could be very old, but because they are so densely packed, none will ever reach its full growth potential. These trees could provide ladders for fire to reach nearby trees.

provide fire ladders to larger surrounding trees during a crown or canopy fire, the most severe type of forest fire.

At points during your saunter through the ponderosa pine forest you may feel as if you have left the forest and entered a meadow with widely spaced trees. This arrangement of trees is referred to as parklike. Although there is no written record describing the Southwest before it was settled by immigrants from the East, low-intensity ground fires that removed accumulated litter and many young trees were more frequent then, effectively keeping the forest more open (see figure 1).

Energy Factories

The flexible, pointed needles of ponderosa pines reach lengths of five to seven inches, making them among the longest in the pine family. Some needles have a slight twist, causing them to show a spiraling pattern. Each bundle of needles, called a fascicle, consists of three (occasionally only two) individual needles. They are lovely to see on a clear day when they glisten in the sunlight. John Muir, founder of the Sierra Club, wrote in 1894 that "this species also gives forth the finest music to the wind.

Plate 19. Ponderosa pine needles on a branch. Each fascicle has three needles. Note the leaf scars along the branch where needles once grew.

Photosynthesis

Photosynthesis is the process through which plants produce their food. Plants obtain carbon dioxide from the atmosphere through tiny openings called stomata that are located on the underside of the leaves and needles. Plants obtain their water from the ground through their roots. Water and carbon dioxide are combined in the presence of chlorophyll, the green pigment in plants, and a chemical reaction powered by light energy from the sun produces sugars and oxygen from the water and carbon dioxide. The plant uses the sugars as food and releases the oxygen into the atmosphere. Animals breathe the oxygen and exhale carbon dioxide into the atmosphere, to be taken up by plants and used in photosynthesis. This is an efficient gas exchange cycle when it remains balanced between respiration and photosynthesis.

The chemical shorthand for the general reaction is:

$$CO_2 + H_2O + sunlight + chlorophyll \rightarrow sugar + O_2$$

After listening to it in all kinds of winds, night and day, season after season, I think I could approximate to my position on the mountains by this pine-music alone."

New needles form from buds on the tips of the terminal shoots, and new growth occurs here, increasing the height of the tree and the length of the branches. As the developing buds elongate during early spring and rise toward the sun, they resemble pale green–and-tan candles. The needles remain on the tree branch for about three years (some reports say as many as five years) before turning brown, at which time they are abscised (released). Look closely and you may see a leaf scar on a branch where fascicles once grew. The brown needles falling now were new three years ago. The abscised needles accumulate as litter on the forest floor, where they slowly decompose over several years and release nutrients into the soil. An excessive litter layer that has not begun to decompose can provide fuel for forest fires and also prevent the establishment of new seedlings.

Just beneath the litter layer is the duff area, where decomposition has begun. The duff layer is subdivided into two regions. The upper duff, sometimes called the fermentation layer, is composed of moderately decomposed needles; the lower duff, known as the humus layer, contains highly decomposed needles and is adjacent to the mineral soil. Carefully pull back some of the litter to observe these layers.

The Rest of the Tree—Alive or Dead?

When you look at a healthy tree, the shimmering green needles and the cones are the only living tissue you see; everything else is dead tissue. That beautiful bark—gray, black, or golden orange— is dead. Even the tree's wooden core, the heartwood, is dead. Between the bark and the heartwood, however, is a layer of living tissue encircling the entire tree that is no more than four milli- meters thick—about the size of the dash in this sentence. This tissue performs several functions crucial for the tree's survival: it produces the bark; it serves as the vascular system that transports the sugar produced in the needles during photosynthesis and the water and nutrients absorbed by the roots to the needles, cones, and buds; and it produces the wooden core of the tree.

This thin living layer of tissue, which extends from the roots to the needles, has four components: cork cambium, phloem, vascular cambium, and xylem. Since this layer is what keeps the tree alive, let's look at it a bit more closely using the cross section of a tree shown in figure 4.

The bark is formed of dead tissue accumulated over the course of many years, perhaps even hundreds of years. It was produced by the cork cambium—the outermost layer of the tree's living tissue. New bark is constantly added to the outside of the cork cambium; thus, the youngest bark is adjacent to the cork cambium and the oldest bark is on the outside of the tree. By adding new layers of bark the cork cambium contributes to the ever-enlarging tree. Thick bark provides fire resistance. Look at an old stump to observe the bark thickness.

The next layer, on the inner side of the cork cambium, is the phloem. The phloem is a one-way street going from the tree's nee- dles to its roots that transports the sugars produced in the needles during photosynthesis. The phloem is produced by the vascular cambium—the layer that lies inside it, toward the core of the tree. The vascular cambium also produces the xylem, the tree's innermost layer of living tissue. Vascular cambium is thus a very valuable tissue for plants because it is responsible for producing the tree's vascular system. The xylem is another one-way street, this one going from bottom to top carrying water and nutrients such as nitrogen, potassium, and phosphorus from the soil to the needles. The xylem also stores some of the sugars produced by photosynthesis in special cells called parenchyma cells. The older xylem is referred to as sapwood, and even though composed of

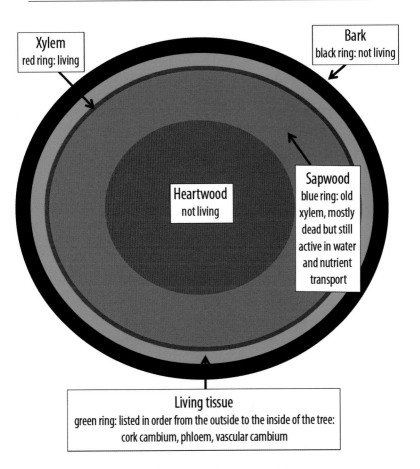

Figure 4. Cross section of a tree (not drawn to scale).

mostly dead tissues, it still functions to transport water and minerals. Sapwood can be several decades old in conifers. As the tree continues to age, the sapwood eventually becomes heartwood, which has no vascular function but does have a high resin content. Thus, both sapwood and heartwood—collectively referred to as wood—are derived from old xylem tissue.

The phloem, vascular cambium, and xylem form the vascular system of the tree. If even a narrow band of this vascular system tissue is removed in a complete circle (i.e., the tree is girdled), the flow of sugars from the needles to the roots through the phloem stops. If a deeper cut is made around the tree, the flow of water through the thin xylem layer and the sapwood to the needles will cease. Girdling inevitably results in the death of the tree. If you have ever come across a dead but still-standing beaver-gnawed tree along a riparian area, then you have seen a girdled tree. American settlers who moved west and built homesteads in thickly forested areas commonly girdled trees and then came back later to chop or cut them down. The notorious bark beetles that have decimated forests from Alaska to Mexico can girdle the trees they infect as they tunnel through, eat, and destroy the phloem. These beetles also introduce fungi that can destroy the phloem and cambium as well as clog the sapwood, stopping water and nutrient movement. Fire can also girdle a tree; fire scars are examples of partial girdling in which the tree survives.

The tree's sapwood and heartwood are the parts we use for lumber. Heart pine lumber, the more highly valued of the two,

Plate 20. Fire scar on the trunk of a ponderosa pine.

is milled directly from heartwood, which in old-growth forests usually has no knots. Lumber from smaller trees is less valued because of its knots—which are actually slices through limbs that were growing along the trunk. Knots do give the wood a distinctive look, especially when used in the interior of a house.

Ponderosas are self-pruning, meaning that the lower branches sometimes die and fall into the litter layer. This occurs often in stands where trees are growing close together and lower limbs are shaded out by the trees around them. Ponderosas that are isolated from other trees keep their lower limbs. Look for this pattern as you saunter.

You may find living trees with very large hollows such as Winnie the Pooh's home in the Hundred Acre Wood. As long as the vascular system is intact, the tree can survive much trauma. Hollow trunks and limbs make good nest sites for birds and den sites for mammals.

Sculptures of the Forest

Standing dead trees are called snags. A snag progresses through numerous stages before it finally topples to the ground. Soon after the tree dies, its green needles turn brown and drop into the litter. Eventually limbs fall and the bark loosens and falls away. Sometimes sections of the upper trunk break off. Ultimately the standing snag succumbs to decay, fungi, and gravity. After falling, the snag enters the final stages of decay, returning the tree's remaining stored nutrients to the forest soil.

Prior to the 1920s, loggers were encouraged to remove snags so that they would not become "lightning rods" for forest fires. It was a common practice to use snags for fuel or wood chips. In Yosemite National Park in 1924, however, park naturalists determined that dead trees were valuable for wildlife nesting and foraging sites and began recommending that snags be preserved. The practice of leaving snags for wildlife has increased since then. In some ponderosa pine forests snags are deliberately created from large trees by girdling.

While leaving snags is positive for wildlife, there are at least two negative aspects of the practice. One is snags' role in spreading fire. When lightning strikes a snag and sets it on fire, the resin-filled heartwood becomes so hot that it explodes, spreading burning debris great distances in the winds created by the fire.

Plate 21. A lone ponderosa pine snag. Note the absence of bark and the broken limbs. This snag provides habitat for cavity-nesting birds, insects, and fungi. Cutting this snag could be dangerous because it might loosen a decaying limb and create a "widowmaker."

Plate 22. A downed ponderosa trunk (foreground) slowly disintegrating into the various elements that were stored inside its tissues. The elements released in the process become available to new plant growth in the forests. Numerous organisms from fungi to ants are involved in the recycling processes.

The second is the potentially hazardous situation firefighters on the ground face when the snags fall or explode. In forests, especially around populated areas or historic buildings that require fire protection, it is prudent to manage the number of snags for those two reasons.

As you examine a snag, look and listen for northern flickers, which use snags for food and shelter. A *rat-a-tat-tat* followed by a pause and then another *rat-a-tat-tat* is a sure sign that one of these large woodpeckers is nearby. Balancing on its specialized feet, with two toes facing forward and two toes backward, and using its stiff tail feathers as a brace, the flicker maneuvers up and down trees, drilling holes with its chisel-like beak. The head moves rapidly back and forth as the flicker pecks the decaying wood in search of wood-eating insects. A thick pad of fat

surrounds and protects the brain from trauma as the bill repeat-
edly hammers into the tree. Once it has exposed them, the flicker
extracts the insects with its very long, barbed, sticky tongue.

Numerous bat species use the loosened bark of snags as roosts.
Wildlife biologists even attach artificial roosts that resemble
loose bark to living trees to encourage bat roosting. Some owls
will nest in cavities excavated by other birds in snags. Hawks
and other raptors use the tops of snags for hunting perches and
nesting sites. Downed logs produced by fallen snags offer shelter
to mice, rabbits, chipmunks, ground squirrels, and skunks, plus
earthworms and numerous insects. The activities of these animals assist in returning the chemical elements stored in the dead
tree back to the forest for reuse by living organisms.

Plate 23. Northern
flicker. This large
woodpecker uses
living and dead
ponderosa pine
trees for nesting
and foraging. (Pho-
tograph by Doug
Iverson. Used with
permission.)

Plate 24. Female northern goshawk feeding young. These raptors
use both deciduous and coniferous trees in old-growth forests.
In the southwestern ponderosa pine forests goshawks feed on
tassel-eared squirrels, other rodents, and rabbits. (Photograph by
David Ponton and Patricia L. Kennedy. Used with permission.)

Plate 25. Long-eared myotis bat. These bats roost in dead trees and feed on insects. (Photograph by Bruce Taubert. Used with permission.)

Plate 26. Spotted bat. Spotted bats also roost in dead trees. They have large ears and white bellies and feed on a variety of insects. (Photograph by Bruce Taubert. Used with permission.)

Pine Scents, Sapsuckers, and Naval Stores

When you first enter the ponderosa pine forest you will surely note its distinctive aroma, especially after a summer monsoon rain when the broken needles release their volatile aromatic scents. For an even more intense aroma, rub your hands on a clump of green needles and sniff. On one of my summer visits to a squirrel study site I was caught in a fifteen-minute hailstorm. The green needles broken by the hailstones released a piney scent that lasted for several hours.

Storm forces are not the only natural source of injuries to ponderosa pine trees. Numerous birds, mammals, and insects can damage the bark. Red-naped sapsuckers drill holes into the bark and sip the sap that fills the holes because it is full of sugars. You will see rows of evenly spaced holes, called sap wells, circling the tree when these woodpeckers have been around. Porcupines scrape the bark from the trunk and branches for food. Insects bore holes through the bark to tap into the phloem.

Plate 27. Red-naped sapsucker. These woodpeckers drill sap wells in the bark and sip the sap and eat the insects that get caught in it. They do not suck the sap, despite their common name. (Photograph by Doug Iverson. Used with permission.)

Plate 28. Sap wells in a yellow-belly ponderosa pine trunk. These tiny holes collect sap and trap insects that become food for sapsuckers.

Trees secrete resins to protect themselves and to seal injured tissues. The chemicals in the resins, which are mainly terpenes, are used in the production of turpentine and rosin (a substance familiar to violinists and gymnasts). These tree products were once used to waterproof seams and joints, and in the general maintenance of wooden sailing ships, and were called naval stores. During the American Civil War, the Union states were cut off from the plentiful pine forests of the South, and naval stores were in short supply. Several turpentine/rosin distilleries constructed in the Sierra Nevada in California for processing ponderosa pines stepped up and supplied the Union Navy with the products it needed.

In the late 1960s samples of ponderosa pine stumps from northern Arizona were sent to a laboratory in Florida to determine whether they still possessed a useful amount of resin. The analysis revealed that indeed there were sufficient resins remaining in the stumps for processing into naval stores.

Resins are said to have medicinal uses as well. In Marguerite Henry's classic children's book *Brighty of the Grand Canyon*, for example, Brighty's caretaker treats the leg wounds the little burro suffered during a mountain lion attack with melted resin from ponderosa pines.

Roots, Underground Fungi, False Truffles, and Mushrooms

Roots are both a tree's anchor and the conduits through which it draws water and nutrients from the soil. They also provide areas for food storage. Lateral roots and taproots are the main types of roots of ponderosas.

The lateral roots of ponderosa pines extend beyond the drip line of the tree in all directions. The drip line is the circular area beneath the longest-extending branches around the canopy of a tree where rain that trickles down the branches strikes the ground. Taproots—roots that extend downward—more than thirty-nine feet long have been documented, but the normal is much less than that, surprising for trees that can grow to be more than two hundred feet tall. When you see an uprooted ponderosa, look at the roots; in many cases you will see rocks incorporated within the root mass.

The lateral roots of ponderosas are home to a variety of hypogeous (underground) fungi that help the tree by increasing the absorptive area of the roots and serving as storage sites for water and nutrients. The tree assists the fungi in turn by providing a place for them to live and by supplying sugars, produced during photosynthesis, for their food. This "mycorrhizal association" (from the Greek *myco* = fungus and *riza* = root; literally "fungus root") benefits both the tree and the fungi. Ecologists refer to this type of relationship as mutualism. Forest researchers have found that trees without mycorrhizal associates are at an extreme disadvantage compared with trees possessing such associates.

Hypogeous fungi produce millions of spores that are locked away beneath the soil in little packages called false truffles. Tree squirrels locate false truffles by smell, dig them out and eat them, and spread the fungi's spores in their fecal pellets, inoculating

Plate 29. Ponderosa pine uprooted by a flash flood at Sunset Crater Volcano National Monument. Note the many long narrow lateral roots and the absence of a long taproot.

Plate 30. A false truffle, *Rhizopogon* sp., found beneath the litter layer attached to the lateral roots of a ponderosa pine. Tassel-eared squirrels feed on such hypogeous fungi and spread their spores throughout the forest in their fecal pellets. (Photograph by J. S. States. Used with permission.)

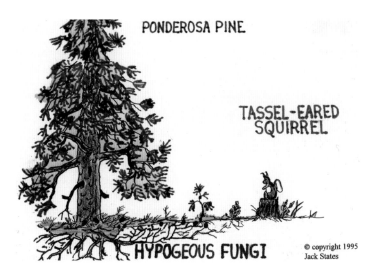

Figure 5. Mutualistic association of tassel-eared squirrels, hypogeous fungi, and ponderosa pine trees. (Drawing by J. S. States. Used with permission.)

other ponderosa roots in the forest. You may observe evidence of the squirrels' digging in the litter. All three members of this mutualistic association benefit: the pine, the squirrel, and the fungi.

If you saunter in the forest after the summer rains you will see an abundance of mushrooms. Each colorful cap is filled with spores that are spread by gravity, wind, and animals. These aboveground fungi are said to be epigeous. Fungi actively turn dead wood from fallen trees, brown needles, and branches back into the chemical elements from which they were formed. They are the recyclers of the forest.

Plate 31. *Amanita muscaria*, an epigeous fungus. Mushrooms are common after summer rains in ponderosa pine forests.

Residents of the Southwestern Ponderosa Pine Forest

A huge suite of organisms resides in the ponderosa pine forest. In addition to fungi and plants you might observe elk, deer, bears, skunks, raccoons, prickly porcupines, soft brown deer mice, ground squirrels, tree squirrels such as the handsome tassel-eared squirrels and the tiny red squirrels, hopping cottontails and jackrabbits, and numerous birds, including the colorful and boastful Steller's jays, wild turkeys, flickers and other woodpeckers, and various raptors. If you are fortunate you will come across an acorn woodpecker's granary tree. When these birds collect acorns, they drive them into the bark of ponderosas for later retrieval, giving the trunk and its branches the appearance of being shot full of holes. Owls and bats are there as well, but they are hidden, sleeping, during your daytime saunters.

Plate 32. An elk in ponderosa forest. (Photograph by Doug Iverson. Used with permission.)

Plate 33. Mule deer resting in a sunny opening in the forest.

Plate 34. A beautiful Steller's jay perched on a rock. The jays feed on Gambel oak acorns buried by tassel-eared squirrels. When jays fly to a ponderosa to perch they use limb-hopping as a means to move upward rather than flying from limb to limb as many other birds do.

Plate 35. Turkeys foraging for seeds and insects beneath a ponderosa pine. They also roost in the pines.

Plate 36. Granary tree of an acorn woodpecker. The birds drill holes in trunks and limbs and stuff an acorn into each hole. Note the many holes in the dead ponderosa pine limb. Beneath this limb were numerous pieces of shelled acorns.

Amphibians and reptiles climb, jump, scamper, and slither across the rocks, tree trunks and stumps, and pine needles. A few species of amphibians live in nearby riparian areas and around water catchments in the forest. Boreal chorus frogs, two species of tree frogs, and northern leopard frogs are among the amphibians that you might see or hear. You might also see a tiger salamander walking about on the forest floor in the early spring or on a rainy summer night. Several species of lizards, including the plateau fence lizard, the mountain short-horned lizard (sometimes mistakenly called a horny toad), the Madrean alligator lizard, several species of skinks, and whiptail lizards, scurry

Plate 37. Greater short-horned lizard. These lizards live in the litter layer of ponderosa pine forests. (Photograph by Erika Novak. Used with permission.)

Plate 38. Black rattlesnake concealed in a ponderosa stump. These very poisonous snakes are found in some ponderosa pine forests in Arizona, where they eat birds, lizards, rabbits, and various rodents. (Photograph by Justin Schofer. Used with permission.)

across the litter layer and along tree trunks in search of food. The gopher snake and several species of whipsnakes, kingsnakes, gartersnakes, and rattlesnakes may also be encountered within the ponderosa pine forests of the Southwest.

In addition to the highly visible vertebrates there are many other seldom-seen residents such as insects, ticks, spiders, harvestmen (also called daddy longlegs), millipedes, and centipedes. More than two hundred species of insects feed on various parts of ponderosas from seeds to roots.

Who Owns the Forests?

Although ponderosa pine forests do occur on private lands, most of them are in national and state parks or in national and state trust lands and forests. Therefore we, the public, own most of the ponderosa pine forests. The forests within the national parks are protected from logging and grazing. National and state forests, in contrast, are managed in a way that allows the commercial use of the forests for sheep and cattle grazing, timber harvesting, and ski resorts, which require tree-cutting for the ski runs. Some of us use the forests for hiking, sauntering, and camping. Some profit from the forest's resources by operating ski resorts, grazing livestock, or harvesting one of the most important timber trees in the United States—the ponderosa. Many of us simply wish to live near the forests for their aesthetic beauty. Certainly it presents a challenge for the forest managers of all agencies to balance the priorities and needs of all those interested in the ponderosa pine forests.

Plate 39. Ponderosa pine trees in Zion National Park, with Checkerboard Mesa in the background.

Tree Scars

Almost all old trees—and many younger ones—have scars. In the 1980s Thomas Swetnam, director of the Laboratory of Tree-Ring Research at the University of Arizona, categorized the types of scars found on tree trunks (Swetnam, 1984). Some tree scars are the result of cultural modifications; others are natural. Examples of cultural modifications include bark peelings by Native Americans for food and target practice, trail blazes to mark paths, and witness trees (trees marked in the 1800s for original land surveys) that surveyors and foresters use for recording specific locations within the forest. Fire, lightning strikes, squirrel and porcupine gnawing, browsing by deer and elk, antler and claw scrapes, and damage done by falling trees and rocks are sources of natural tree scars.

An example of a tree scar left by Native Americans can be found at Ivikukuch, or Target Tree Camp, in the San Juan National Forest near Mancos, Colorado. The informational sign at the site states: "When the Utes camped here they would use an old tree for bow and rifle target practice during hunting expeditions. They

Plate 40. A ponderosa pine sapling with an antler-rubbing scar made by deer or elk.

Plate 41. Culturally modified ponderosa pine tree at Target Tree Campground, San Juan National Forest, near Mancos, Colorado.

also scraped sweet sap and the cambium from ponderosa pines. The sap was made into a kind of candy. The cambium was used in soups, stews, and for making a tea. Many of the old yellow or red barked ponderosas here still show large, oval shaped scars left by this use."

A triangular, blackened "cat face" scar at the base of an old ponderosa, such as the one shown in plate 20, is a sign that the tree survived a fire long ago. Notice the margin around the cat face where the tree has grown a callus for protection. Fire scars, depending on their age, can be covered by the callus and show accumulations of resin. Researchers can reconstruct the fire history of a forest by examining fire scars.

Uses of Ponderosas from Past to Present

The ancient Pueblo Indians of the southwestern United States used ponderosa pine logs as beams in the construction of their dwellings and kivas. The timbers were cut and hauled (without wheels!) from forests many miles away. An excellent example of this type of construction is at Chaco Culture National Historical Park in northwestern New Mexico. The logs in the ancient structures there were harvested from the Chuska Mountains, more than fifty miles west of Chaco.

Logging of the ponderosa forests began during the late 1880s to meet the nation's growing demand for lumber. New settlements

Plate 42. Ponderosa pine log in a wall at Pueblo Bonito at Chaco Culture National Historical Park in New Mexico. This area was occupied between about A.D. 800 and A.D. 1200.

Plate 43. Pile of logs that will be milled into lumber.

in the Southwest needed timber for railroad ties; bridges over creeks, rivers, and canyons; mine-shaft supports; houses, businesses, corrals, and mills; and firewood. During World War II, ponderosa pine wood found its way to the European and Pacific theaters in the form of ammunition crates. Today, dimensional lumber, such as the ubiquitous two-by-fours and two-by-sixes used in framing houses and the heavy logs used in post and beam construction, are often from ponderosa pines.

As you saunter through the forests you will see the stumps of harvested trees. Some of these are very old and are valuable sources of historical data pertaining to past harvesting and tree densities. Before loggers used chain saws and mechanical harvesters with huge and powerful hydraulic jaws, they cut down trees with axes or, more likely, with two-person crosscut saws. Old stumps that are two or more feet above the soil rather than at ground level are signs that the tree was taken down with a crosscut saw. The lumberjacks cut at a height that made it easier to push and pull the huge, cumbersome saws. A very high stump may be a sign that the tree was cut in the winter in deep snow. Cutting in winter did offer benefits to the lumberjacks because the logs could be skidded out from the forests over the snow or ice—a process sometimes called snaking out—by mule and horse teams, with the snow offering a smooth surface and less friction than the bare ground of summer.

Plate 44. High-cut stumps. Chest-height stumps were common in the days of crosscut saws because that was a comfortable height for the pull and push between the two lumberjacks operating the saw. Depth of snow was also a factor in the cutting height. Today trees are cut at ground level.

Plant Neighbors

Many of the trees that live in association with or near ponderosas are other conifers such as Douglas-fir, spruces, junipers such as alligator juniper (so named for its alligator hide–like bark), pinyon, and limber pines. Although ancient bristlecone pines are found at higher elevations and do not normally grow near ponderosa pines, there are some bristlecones intermingled with ponderosas in the San Francisco Peaks near Flagstaff, Arizona. Other species grow interspersed within the ponderosas as well. Large stands of quaking aspen are especially beautiful in their golden fall attire. Clusters of Gambel oak with their bright green, lobed leaves and brown-capped green acorns provide food for deer, turkeys, squirrels, and Steller's jays. In some areas the compound leaves and deep pink flowers of New Mexico locust trees offer a striking contrast to the deep green needles of the ponderosas.

Understory plants include grasses such as mountain muhly, squirreltail, and Arizona fescue; and shrubs such as buckbrush, Oregon grape, cliffrose, wax currant, and Apache plume. Louseworts, various penstemons, numerous types of yellow composite flowers (look for flowers that have a sunflower-like face),

Plate 45. Mullein growing in a sunny opening surrounded by grasses and ponderosa pine trees. The central stalk can be six feet tall and is loaded with yellow flowers that produce tiny black seeds. The soft leaves have been called "cowboy/girl toilet tissue."

Plate 46. Woodland pinedrops. These plants have no chlorophyll and parasitize conifer roots to get the nutrients they need. During the fall the plants dry out and turn rusty brown. The genus name, *Pterospora*, means "winged seed."

pinedrops (a parasitic plant), thistles, various buckwheats, dwarf irises, wild geraniums, and other wildflowers provide an ever-changing color palette beneath the towering pines during the spring, summer, and fall.

Mistletoe and Witches' Brooms

Dwarf mistletoe (which is not the familiar mistletoe we hang during holidays) is a parasite on ponderosa pine trees. The plant sinks rootlike structures through the bark, penetrating the phloem and stealing the sugars produced by the pine. Dwarf mistletoe stunts the ponderosa's growth, distorts its shape, weakens its defenses against other diseases and infections, and can even kill the tree. The distorted branches, called witches' brooms, serve as platforms for nests of birds and squirrels. These same platforms can act as ladders for fire to spread from lower branches to the upper parts of a tree during forest fires. Dwarf mistletoe produces sticky seeds that can be transmitted from an infected tree to a healthy tree when they are ejected into the air or adhere to the feathers or fur and feet of birds and mammals as the animals move through the forest. If you observe a tree with a mistletoe infection, look around at other nearby trees, which are also likely to be infected. Mule deer and tassel-eared squirrels eat the tender shoots of dwarf mistletoe.

Plate 47. Dwarf mistletoe. This parasite infects the trunk and branches of ponderosas, sinking rootlike structures into the phloem to obtain nutrients produced by the tree. The tiny, sticky fruits can be spread to other ponderosas on birds' feet.

Plate 48. Witches' broom caused by dwarf mistletoe infection. The distorted growths catch falling debris, and various animals use them for nest and resting sites.

Mistletoe Infection Classification System (modified from Hawksworth, 1977)

To determine the degree of mistletoe infection, face the tree and visually divide the crown horizontally into thirds. Rate each third separately as 0 (no infection), 1 (half or fewer of the branches in the third are infected), or 2 (more than half the branches in the third are infected); then total the numbers for the three sections.

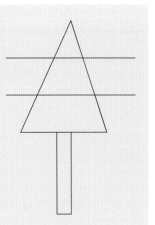

A Bit of Geology

Ponderosa pines grow in soils produced by all three of the recognized parent rock types. These soils vary widely in their mineral content, thickness, and pH.

Cinder- and lava-based soils are abundant in northern Arizona, and the largest contiguous ponderosa pine forest in the world grows there. At Sunset Crater Volcano National Monument in northern Arizona, bizarrely shaped ponderosas grow in the red cinders and in the sharp-edged pahoehoe and aa lavas left behind from an eruption that occurred more than nine hundred years ago. In nearby Walnut Canyon National Monument

The Three Rock Types of the Earth

Igneous rocks are produced by tremendous temperatures and pressures deep within the Earth's crust. Examples: cinders, lava, basalt, and granite.

Sedimentary rocks are produced by sediments that were carried to a site by wind or water. Examples: sandstone and limestone.

Metamorphic rocks are produced from igneous and sedimentary rocks that have been altered by high temperature and great pressure. Examples: limestone changes into marble and sandstone into quartzite.

and Grand Canyon National Park, ponderosas grow in ancient, fossil-rich Kaibab limestone. In southern Utah, ponderosas grow between sandstone cracks in the 2,300-foot-thick Navajo sandstone in Zion National Park. In Bryce Canyon National Park ponderosas grow among the pink-orange hoodoos formed from the iron-rich Claron Formation. An especially good place to see towering ponderosas rising toward the tops of Bryce's stately hoodoos is along a section of the Navajo Loop Trail known as "Wall Street." In parts of Colorado and northern New Mexico, ponderosas grow in soils formed from basalt, quartzite, and granite from the Rocky Mountains. Ponderosas grow in sedimentary and igneous rocks at Mesa Verde National Park. If you visit Devils Tower National Monument in Wyoming, note that ponderosas ring the base of that massive basalt tower.

Bark Beetles

Bark beetles, tiny insects that resemble an elongated BB, are a natural part of the ponderosa pine ecosystem. Usually the beetles are present in relatively small numbers, but on occasion population numbers skyrocket, and large areas of the forest are quickly killed. Trees already under stress are most susceptible to bark beetles. Outbreaks happen most commonly during extended drought, when stressed trees cannot produce enough resin to resist the overwhelming multitudes of these tiny phloem feeders. Other stressors include high stand density of trees, pathogenic fungal infections, lightning strikes, various root diseases, defoliating insect infestations, and dwarf mistletoe infections. Healthy, unstressed trees can mount an effective defense by producing copious amounts of resin, which plugs the holes the female beetles create on entry, effectively "pitching" the beetle out of the tree.

Bark beetles complete part of their life cycle under the bark. Gravid (bearing fertilized eggs) females burrow beneath the bark and lay their eggs, which hatch into larvae. The larvae tunnel beneath the bark, devouring the phloem. Once the larvae have girdled the tree, it will die. The larvae create distinctive paths, or galleries, as they feed. Different species of bark beetles create distinctive gallery shapes, which can be used to identify them. As you saunter through the forest look for these galleries, which resemble multibranched tunnels, on standing dead trees or downed trunks that have missing bark. The galleries can also

Plate 49. Bark beetle. These forest pests are only about one-fourth inch long. The larvae feed on phloem tissues, and large infestations can kill ponderosas. (Photograph by Rich Hofstetter. Used with permission.)

Plate 50. Bark beetle galleries beneath the bark of a ponderosa pine tree. (Photograph by Rich Hofstetter. Used with permission.)

be observed on the underside of the bark that has fallen from the dead tree. Bark beetles are food for birds such as brown creepers, nuthatches, and woodpeckers.

Studies conducted by F. P. Keen in the 1940s that examined the tree's age, crown size, and position within a stand of trees clearly showed that older ponderosas with poor canopies and reduced growth rates were four times more likely to be killed by bark beetles than younger trees with full canopies. Thus, in addition to drought conditions and other stresses, overall age and level of vigor of a tree are important factors that predispose ponderosas to beetle attacks.

Plate 51. A ponderosa pine tree girdled and killed by bark beetles.

Beetles pick up fungal spores in their movements and carry them along when they invade the tree. Signs of a fungal infection are a bluish discoloration on cut ends of stumps, logs, or limbs spreading from the bark inward to the center of the tree that was caused by the fungal hyphae (rootlike structures). The fungus blocks the xylem and sapwood, eventually causing the tree's death. The fungus does not affect the strength of the wood, and blue-stained wood is common at lumberyards.

Other Insects and Fungi

In addition to bark beetles, a number of other beetles, moths, aphids, and scale insects attack ponderosa pine trees, as do numerous fungi. Every part of the tree from seeds to roots holds some particular nutritional interest for insects and fungi. Some team up, forming a mutualistic relationship, as the already mentioned bark beetle and the blue stain fungus do. The bark beetles carry the fungus into the tree. The fungus blocks the production of resin that the tree uses to defend against the beetle infection. Both the beetle and the fungus benefit from the association. The tree eventually dies.

The larvae of Pandora moths and ponderosa pine budworms consume young needles. The Paiute Indians of California still collect and eat Pandora moth larvae, which they call *piuga*. Larvae of the western pine-shoot borer moth tunnel through the center of new growth. Ponderosa pine seedworm moth larvae consume seeds inside the closed cones. Phloem feeders such as the black pineleaf scale insects and aphids pierce the plant tissues and suck the sugars from the needles, which die and turn brown on the branches. Fungi with such unusual names as needle blight, gall rust, root rot, and heart rot also infect ponderosa pine trees.

Fire and Flood

Before Euro-Americans actively began to settle the southwestern United States in the early 1870s, frequent forest fires reduced accumulated litter and clustered seedlings, creating open, park-like forests with abundant native grasses and wildflowers. The pioneers' cattle and sheep reduced the native grasses that had supplied fuel for those low-intensity ground fires. Settlers suppressed fires to protect their homes and ranches. Without periodic low-intensity ground fires, needle and branch litter built up beneath the trees. That concentrated litter provided fuel for much hotter fires. Unthinned pine seedlings grew into thick stands that provided ladders for fires to spread into the upper crowns of older ponderosas.

Every year lightning starts hundreds of forest fires. Old ponderosas, with their thick fire-resistant bark, may survive many fires, but they are also filled with volatile resins and will literally explode during the hottest fires, throwing sparks for hundreds of yards. Fire season is the most dreaded time for those who live near the forest. In addition to lightning strikes the forests are now at the mercy of humans, whether campers who carelessly leave a campfire, or smokers who thoughtlessly toss their cigarette butts into the forest, or arsonists.

During the summer of 2002 in east-central Arizona, the Rodeo fire, started by an arsonist, merged with the Chediski fire, which was started by a stranded motorist. The combined Rodeo-Chediski fires consumed more than 468,000 acres. Nine years later the Wallow fire, started accidentally when two campers mismanaged their campfire, burned 538,000 acres in eastern Arizona and western New Mexico. Floods followed both fires.

In the summer of 2010 a very careless human left a campfire unattended. The resulting Schultz fire burned fifteen thousand acres of trees on the San Francisco Peaks near Flagstaff and threatened hundreds of homes. Firefighters from across the country fought the fire for days and saved every home. Exactly a month later, when the heavy summer monsoons began, the dead trees on the denuded, blackened mountainsides could not hold the soil in place, and torrents of rock-filled mud rushed into the homes below. Floodwaters filled the streets, leaving behind burned limbs, tree trunks, and boulders. Tragically, two young girls drowned when the rushing waters eroded an embankment along one of the many outlet channels.

It is the role of the Forest Service to manage the forests to minimize such devastating events. Forest Service managers determine when to ban campfires and close national forests to camping and other recreation because dry, windy conditions create a high risk of fire. The Forest Service also conducts "prescribed" burns—sometimes called "controlled burns"—in areas with thickly built-up litter and small unhealthy trees to reduce the kindling available for much larger catastrophic fires. Prescribed burns should only be conducted when weather conditions reduce the chance of the fire becoming unmanaged and spreading. An example of an "out-of-control" prescribed burn was the Cerro Grande fire around Los Alamos, New Mexico, in 2000. High winds and drought circumstances spread the fire over forty-eight thousand acres. The huge quantities of fuels that have accumulated in the ponderosa pine forests of the southwestern United States mandate an increase in controlled burns, but only when conditions are favorable.

Since the late 1980s, ecological restoration of ponderosa pine forests in northern Arizona and the Colorado Plateau has been

Plate 52. Schultz fire, Flagstaff, Arizona, summer 2010. Photograph taken from the author's neighborhood. Note the orange glow of exploding yellowbelly ponderosas.

a major research project in the School of Forestry at Northern
Arizona University (NAU) in Flagstaff, which is situated within
the largest contiguous ponderosa pine forest in the world. Wally
Covington, a Regent's Professor in the School of Forestry, and his
colleagues at NAU began this research. Over the years the researchers have examined hundreds of fire scars on living trees and old
stumps to reconstruct the fire history of ponderosa pine forests. It
was this research that determined that ponderosa pine forests in the
Southwest were once subject to frequent low-intensity ground fires.

A hundred years of fire suppression has created forests much
denser than those of the past. The ponderosa pine forest near
the San Francisco Peaks that C. Hart Merriam and Leonhard
Stejneger surveyed in the 1890s (see figure 1) was open and

Plate 53. Fire-scarred stump. These remnants can provide
valuable data to researchers reconstructing fire histories
within ponderosa pine forests.

parklike, with clumps of old trees and widely spaced younger trees. Ponderosa pine forests in the southwestern United States today have many more small trees growing in dense clusters, and are thus more fire prone. Large accumulations of downed limbs and discarded needles add to the problem. Without some thinning of the smaller trees, thereby reducing limbs that serve as fire ladders into the upper canopies of older trees, and the reduction of the packed litter layer, catastrophic wildfires that can actually replace whole stands of trees covering hundreds of square miles will continue to burn southwestern forests.

The problem is not insoluble. Ponderosa pine forests similar to those Merriam and Stejneger saw can be restored by selective thinning of dense stands and prescribed burns to reduce the fuel load. John Muir prescribed perhaps the best solution in a speech he gave before the Sierra Club: "Few are altogether deaf to the preaching of pine trees. Their sermons on the mountains go to our hearts; and if people in general could be got into the woods, even for once, to hear the trees speak for themselves, all difficulties in the way of forest preservation would vanish." *

Climate Change—It's Real

Climate change is irrefutable. Atmospheric temperatures are increasing. Ocean water temperatures are increasing. Glaciers, snowfields, and polar icecaps are melting. There is drought where drought has been rare and increased flooding where flooding has been rare. Large tropical storms, increased snowfalls in some areas and decreased snowfalls in others, decreased snow retention, and warmer temperatures earlier and later than usual are warning signs that our global climate is changing. Certainly the Earth has experienced warming and cooling cycles since its origin, but the current anthropogenic contributions of greenhouse gases are unquestionably increasing global atmospheric temperatures.

The Earth is enveloped in a blanket of gases that absorb heat and warm the surface, effectively creating an enormous greenhouse. These gases include water vapor, carbon dioxide,

---

* John Muir, "The National Parks and Forest Reservations" (speech to the Sierra Club, November 23, 1895), *Sierra Club Bulletin* 1 (7) (1896): 271–84, at 282–83.

methane, and nitrous oxides. Though carbon dioxide is only a minor component of the greenhouse gases, CO_2 levels in the atmosphere are of critical concern. Carbon dioxide is essential for plants to perform photosynthesis, and it is released naturally through respiration, lightning-caused forest fires, and volcanic eruptions. The activities of humans, however, mainly through our increased use of fossil fuels, have increased the amount of carbon dioxide in the atmosphere to dangerous levels, which, combined with large-scale deforestation, are creating an imbalance that has contributed to climate change and threatens the future of our planet.

Trees take carbon dioxide from the atmosphere and incorporate it into cellulose (wood), thus removing the gas and storing the carbon within the tree's tissues. Forests are in a real sense "carbon banks." When trees are cut or destroyed by fire, the size of the planet's carbon bank diminishes. It seems obvious that forests should be replanted so that carbon sequestration will continue. Burning fossil fuels releases carbon dioxide into the atmosphere. Like deforestation, huge fires that destroy landscape-size chunks of trees remove ever more photosynthetic surfaces and also release more carbon dioxide into the atmosphere. The increased carbon dioxide traps ever more heat. Our greenhouse is changing; it is out of balance.

We must intervene if we are to slow or halt the catastrophic changes that appear to be in store for our home, our Earth. Replanting forests helps to mediate carbon dioxide levels in the atmosphere because the trees sequester the carbon, but much more needs to be done. The United States must set an example by moving aggressively into the use of renewable sources to satisfy our energy needs.

The Beginning (Not "The End")

A leisurely saunter in a ponderosa pine forest should fill your senses with sounds, colors, textures, and smells. As you walked this day, you heard the wind blowing through the treetops and the sounds of the animals that call the ponderosa forests home. You heard and felt the crunch of brown needles beneath your feet. You saw green needles and cones, golden-orange bark, yellow pollen cones, and blackened fire scars. Your eyes feasted on the brilliant panorama of wildflowers. If you were observant and

Plate 54. A saunter in a ponderosa pine forest.

in the forest during the right time, you saw winged seeds and tiny seedlings. Maybe you paused to examine a pinecone and saw the fascinating mathematical arrangement of its bracts. You may have counted the growth rings of a stump to determine how old the tree was when it was cut.

You observed the collective contributions of the myriad tiny creatures and numerous fungi that assist in the decomposition of the brown needles, old limbs, and downed trunks on the forest floor. You allowed your fingers to explore the deep furrows of the yellowbelly pines as you smelled the aromas of kitchen spices exuding from the bark. You learned to identify blackjacks and yellowbellies and squirrel digs. You spotted witches' brooms and sap wells created by sap- and insect-eating birds.

You now understand how fragile and yet how strong the massive ponderosa is. You know the forests are yours to enjoy and to protect. Now you are ready to begin your own saunters through the forest. Take friends and show them the true delights of sauntering in a ponderosa pine forest.

In every walk with nature one receives far more than he seeks.*

---

* John Muir. *Steep Trails California—Utah—Nevada—Washington—Oregon—The Grand Canyon*, chap. 9, Mormon lilies, ed. William Frederic Bade, May 1918.

Taxonomy and Scientific Name of the Ponderosa Pine

Domain: Eukarya, organisms with a membrane-bound nucleus
  Kingdom: Plantae, plants
    Subkingdom: Tracheobionta, vascular plants
      Superdivision: Spermatophyta, seed plants
        Division: Coniferophyta, conifers
          Class: Pinopsida
            Order: Pinales
              Family: Pinaceae, pine family
                Genus: *Pinus*, pine (C. Linnaeus 1753)
                  Subgenus: *Pinus*
                    Section: *Pinus*
                      Subsection: *Ponderosae*
                        species: *ponderosa* (Douglas ex. C. Lawson)*
                          Varieties: var. *ponderosa* (Pacific ponderosa pine); var. *scopulorum* (Rocky Mountain ponderosa pine); and var. *arizonica*.

Ponderosa pine is listed within three forest types in the western United States by the Society of American Foresters:

1. Type 237: Interior Ponderosa Pine (most widespread of the three ponderosa pine forest types)
2. Type 244: Ponderosa Pine–Douglas-Fir
3. Type 245: Pacific Ponderosa Pine

---

* The scientific name of the ponderosa pine is *Pinus ponderosa* Dougl. ex C. Lawson. This indicates that David Douglas (Dougl.) assigned the name to a specimen he collected. This was documented in the journal Douglas kept from 1823 to 1827 during his travels in North America, but his description was never formally published in any scientific paper. When Charles Lawson (Laws.) and his father, Peter, published the name and description they credited it to Douglas.

Checklist of Some of the Mammals in Southwestern Ponderosa Pine Forests

Mammal field guide suggestion: M. Elbrock, *Mammal Tracks and Sign: A Guide to North American Species* (Mechanicsburg, PA: Stackpole Books, 2003), 779 pp.

Name of Mammal	Date Observed	Additional Info
Abert's squirrel*		
Arizona gray squirrel		
Black-tailed jackrabbit		
Bobcat		
Cottontail rabbit		
Coyote		
Elk		
Golden-mantled ground squirrel		
Gray fox		
Kaibab squirrel*		
Long-eared myotis		
Mountain lion		
Mule deer		
Pocket gopher		
Porcupine		
Raccoon		
Red squirrel		
Rock squirrel		
Spotted bat		
Spotted skunk		
Striped skunk		

* Both are tassel-eared squirrels.

Checklist of Some of the Birds of the Southwestern Ponderosa Pine Forests

Bird field guide suggestions: D. A. Sibley, *The Sibley Field Guide to Birds of Western North America* (New York: Alfred A. Knopf, 2003), 472 pp.; J. L. Dunn and J. Alderfer, eds., *National Geographic Field Guide to the Birds of North America*, 6th ed. (Washington, DC: National Geographic Society, 2011), 574 pp.

Name of Bird	Date Observed	Additional Info
Acorn woodpecker		
American robin		
Broad-tailed hummingbird		
Brown creeper		
Common raven		
Dark-eyed junco		
Hairy woodpecker		
Hermit thrush		
House wren		
Mountain chickadee		
Mourning dove		
Northern flicker		
Northern goshawk		
Pine siskin		
Pygmy nuthatch		
Red crossbill		
Red-naped sapsucker		
Red-tailed hawk		
Steller's jay		
Western bluebird		
Western tanager		
White-breasted nuthatch		
Yellow-rumped warbler		

Brief History of the Establishment and Responsibilities of the U.S. Forest Service

Motto of the U.S. Forest Service (USFS): "Caring for the land and serving people."

1876   The U.S. Congress formed the Office of Special Agent in the Department of Agriculture to evaluate the conditions of the forests in the United States. In 1901 this office became the Division of Forestry.

1891   The Forest Reserve Act empowered the president to establish forest reserves on public domain lands.

1897   The Organic Act gave the U.S. Department of the Interior and U.S. Geological Survey the authority to manage forest reserves while providing a continuous timber supply for the nation.

1901   The Division of Forestry was established within the Department of Agriculture.

1905   The U.S. Forest Service was created within the Department of Agriculture.

1905–1910   Gifford Pinchot served as first chief of the Forest Service during the Theodore Roosevelt administration. He later was a two-term governor of Pennsylvania and a well-known spokesperson for conservation ethics and efforts.

1960   The Multiple Use Sustained Yield Act added additional management priorities to the USFS such as recreation, fish and wildlife, grazing, minerals, water, and wilderness management.

1964   The Wilderness Act defined wilderness: "A wilderness, in contrast with those areas where man and his own works dominate the landscape, is hereby recognized as an area where the earth and community of life are untrammeled by man, where man himself is a visitor who does not remain." Under this act thirty-five million acres of wilderness land would eventually be protected.

1970 The National Environmental Policy Act (NEPA) was the first major environmental law enacted by Congress that aligned USFS decisions with NEPA environmental guidelines.

1973 The Endangered Species Act provided for the conservation of endangered and threatened species of fish, wildlife, and plants and caused the USFS to address endangered and threatened species that might be living within proposed timber sales.

1974 The Forest and Rangeland Renewable Resources Planning Act required the secretary of agriculture to assess the nation's renewable resources every ten years.

1976 The National Forest Management Act addressed the forests of the United States as renewable resources and stressed a complete assessment of present and anticipated demands, uses, and supplies of forests with respect to the 1960 Multiple Use Sustained Yield Act.

1978 The Cooperative Forestry Assistance Act revised the authority of the USFS with regard to rural development, forest products, conservation, recycling, watershed restoration, and enhancement, both tribal and domestic.

Suggested Readings

Brennan, T. C., and A. T. Holycross. 2006. *A Field Guide to Amphibians and Reptiles in Arizona*. Phoenix: Arizona Game and Fish Department. 152 pp.

Darrow, K. 2006. *Wild about Wildflowers*. Glendale, AZ: Wildcat Publishing Company. 224 pp.

Degenhardt, W. G., C. W. Painter, and A. H. Price. 1996. *Amphibians and Reptiles in New Mexico*. Albuquerque: University of New Mexico Press. 507 pp.

Douglass, A. E. 1929. The secret of the Southwest solved by talkative tree rings. *National Geographic* 56 (6): 736–70.

Dunn, J. L., and J. Alderfer, eds. *National Geographic Field Guide to the Birds of North America*, 6th ed. Washington, DC: National Geographic Society, 2011. 574 pp.

Elbrock, M. 2003. *Mammal Tracks and Sign: A Guide to North American Species*. Mechanicsburg, PA: Stackpole Books. 779 pp.

Farjon, A. 2008. *A Natural History of Conifers*. Portland, OR: Timber Press. 304 pp.

Friederici, P. 2003. *Ecological Restoration of Southwestern Ponderosa Pine Forests*. Washington, DC: Island Press. 584 pp.

Jackson, J. P. 1979. *The Biography of a Tree*. Middle Village, NY: Jonathan David Publishers. 199 pp.

Mills, E. A. 1914. *The Story of a Thousand-Year Pine*. Boston: Houghton Mifflin. 64 pp.

Muir, J. 1894. *The Mountains of California*. New York: New Century. 389 pp.

———. 1911. *My First Summer in the Sierra*. Cambridge, MA: Riverside Press. 160 pp.

Murie, O. J. 1998. *A Field Guide to Animal Tracks*. Boston: Houghton Mifflin Harcourt. 375 pp.

Murphy, A. 1994. *Graced by Pines—the Ponderosa Pine in the American West*. Missoula, MT: Mountain Press. 119 pp.

Palmer, A. W. 1911. *The Mountain Trail and Its Message*. Boston: Pilgrim Press. Reprint, Fresno, CA: Sixth Street Press, 1997. 31 pp.

Sibley, D. A. *The Sibley Field Guide to Birds of Western North America*. New York: Alfred A. Knopf, 2003. 472 pp.

Spellenberg, R. 1979. *The Audubon Society Field Guide to North American Wildflowers. Western Region*. New York: Alfred A. Knopf. 864 pp.

States, J. S. 1990. *Mushrooms and Truffles of the Southwest*. Tucson: University of Arizona Press. 234 pp.

Wheelwright, J. 2006. Fire in the sky: Why America's ecological treasures sometimes just need to burn. *Discover* magazine (June).

Literature Consulted

Many of the papers and websites listed below have huge numbers of references for the curious reader. Some references are listed in more than one category.

Amphibians, Lizards, and Snakes of Ponderosa Pine Forests

Brennan, T. C., and A. T. Holycross. 2006. *A Field Guide to Amphibians and Reptiles in Arizona*. Phoenix: Arizona Game and Fish Department. 152 pp.

Degenhardt, W. G., C. W. Painter, and A. H. Price. 1996. *Amphibians and Reptiles in New Mexico*. Albuquerque: University of New Mexico Press. 431 pp.

Germaine, S. S., and H. L. Germaine. 2003. Lizard distributions and reproductive succession in a ponderosa pine forest. *Journal of Herpetology* 37 (4): 645–52.

Birds of the Ponderosa Pine Forests

Bassett, R. L., D. A. Boyce Jr., M. H. Reiser, R. T. Graham, and R. T. Reynolds. 1994. Influence of site quality and stand density on goshawk habitat in southwestern forests. *Studies in Avian Biology* 16: 41–45.

Covert-Bratland, T., C. Theimer, and W. M. Block. 2007. Hairy woodpecker winter roost characteristics in burned ponderosa pine forest. *Wilson Journal of Ornithology* 111 (1): 43–52.

Farris, K. L., M. J. Huss, and S. Zack. 2004. The role of foraging woodpeckers in the decomposition of ponderosa pine snags. *Condor* 106 (1): 50–59.

Ffolliott, P. F., C. L. Stropki, H. Chen, and D. G. Neary. 2009. Observations of bird numbers and species following a historic wildfire in Arizona ponderosa pine forests. *Journal of the Arizona-Nevada Academy of Science* 41 (1): 16–23.

Gaines, W. L., M. Haggard, J. F. Lehmkuhl, A. L. Lyons, and R. J. Harrod. 2007. Short-term response of land birds to ponderosa pine restoration. *Restoration Ecology* 15 (4): 670–78.

Ganey, J. L., and S. C. Vojta. 2004. Characteristics of snags containing excavated cavities in northern Arizona mixed-conifer and ponderosa pine forests. *Forest Ecology and Management* 199: 323–32.

Griffis-Kyle, K. L., and P. Beier. 2002. Small isolated aspen stands enrich bird communities in southwestern ponderosa pine forests. *Biological Conservation* 110: 375–85.

Grinnell, J., and T. I. Storer. 1924. *Animal Life in the Yosemite. An Account of the Mammals, Birds, Reptiles, and Amphibians in a Cross Section of the Sierra Nevada.* Berkeley: University of California Press. 752 pp.

Hall, L. S., M. L. Morrison, and W. M. Block. 1997. Songbird status and roles. In *Songbird Ecology in Southwestern Ponderosa Pine Forests: A Literature Review.* USDA Forest Service General Technical Report RM-GTR-292, tech. eds. W. M. Block and D. M. Finch. 19 pp.

Jentsch, S., R. W. Mannan, B. G. Dicken, and W. M. Block. 2007. Associations among breeding birds and Gambel oak in southwestern ponderosa pine forests. *Journal of Wildlife Management* 72 (4): 994–1000.

Ligon, J. D. 1973. Foraging behavior of the white-headed woodpecker in Idaho. *Auk* 90: 862–69.

Lundquist, J. E., and R. M. Reich. 2006. Tree diseases, canopy structure, and bird distributions in ponderosa pine forests. *Journal of Sustainable Forestry* 23 (2): 17–45.

Merriam, C. H., and L. Stejneger. 1890. *Results of a Biological Survey of the San Francisco Mountain Region and the Desert of the Little Colorado, Arizona.* North American Fauna 3. Washington, DC: U.S. Department of Agriculture, Division of Ornithology and Mammalia. 136 pp.

Mills, T. R., M. A. Rumble, and L. D. Flake. 2000. Habitat of birds in ponderosa pine and aspen/birch forest in the Black Hills, South Dakota. *Journal of Field Ornithology* 71 (2): 187–206.

Mooney, K. A. 2007. Tritrophic effects of birds and ants on a canopy food web, tree growth, and phytochemistry. *Ecology* 88 (8): 2005–14.

Oliver, W. W. 1970. The feeding pattern of sapsuckers on ponderosa pine in northeastern California. *Condor* 72 (2): 241.

Patton, D. R. 1997. *Wildlife Habitat Relationships in Forested Ecosystems.* 2nd ed. Portland, OR: Timber Press. 502 pp.

Purcell, K. L., and D. A. Drynan. 2006. Use of hardwoods by birds nesting in ponderosa pine forests. In *Today's Challenges, Tomorrow's Opportunities.* Proceedings of the Sixth California Oak Symposium, October 9–12, 2006, Rohnert Park, CA.

Raish, C., W. Yong, and J. Marzluff. 1997. Contemporary human use of southwestern ponderosa pine forests. In *Songbird Ecology in Southwestern Ponderosa Pine Forests: A Literature Review.* USDA Forest Service General Technical Report RM-GTR-292, tech. eds. W. M. Block and D. M. Finch. 14 pp.

Reynolds, R. T., and B. D. Linkhart. 1992. Flammulated owls in ponderosa pine: Evidence of preference for old growth. Paper presented at workshop on OM-growth forests in the Southwest and Rocky Mountain Region, Portal, AZ.

Rosenstock, S. S. 1996. *Habitat Relationships of Breeding Birds in Northern Arizona Ponderosa Pine and Pine-Oak Forests, a Final Report*. Research Branch Technical Report 23. Arizona Department of Fish and Game, Phoenix.

Scott, V. E. 1978. Characteristics of ponderosa pine snags used by cavity-nesting birds in Arizona. *Journal of Forestry* 76 (1): 26–28.

Smith, C. C., and R. P. Balda. 1979. Competition among insects, birds, and mammals for conifer seeds. *American Zoologist* 19: 1065–83.

Smith, C. F., and S. E. Aldous. 1947. The influence of mammals and birds in retarding artificial and natural reseeding of coniferous forests in the United States. *Journal of Forestry* 45: 361–69.

Stallcup, P. L. 1968. Spatio-temporal relationships of nuthatches and woodpeckers in ponderosa pine forests of Colorado. *Ecology* 49 (5): 831–43.

———. 1969. Hairy woodpeckers feeding on pine seeds. *Auk* 86: 134–35.

Szaro, R., and R. P. Balda. 1979. Bird Community Dynamics in a Ponderosa Pine Forest. *Studies in Avian Biology* 3: 1–66.

Tevis, L. Jr. 1953. Effects of vertebrate animals on seed crops of sugar pine. *Journal of Wildlife Management* 17 (2): 128–31.

Vierling, K. T., and D. J. Gentry. 2008. Red-headed woodpecker density and productivity in relation to time since fire in burned pine forests. *Fire Ecology*, special issue, 4 (1): 15–25.

Wakeling, B. F., S. Weimann, T. Jackson, B. Dowler, M. Eacret, and J. Gillis. 1996. Ponderosa pine tree selection by roosting Merriam's turkeys in north-central Arizona. In *Proceedings of the Biennial Conference on Research on the Colorado Plateau*, pp. 119–24.

Yasuda, S. 2010. California partners in flight coniferous bird conservation plan for the flammulated owl. USDA Forest Service, Eldorado National Forest, Placerville Ranger District, Camino, CA.

Young, M. T. 1999. Owls in small packages. http://hdl.handle.net/10176/co:3496.

Climate Change Related to Ponderosa Pine Ecology

Ganey, J. L., and S. C. Vojta. 2011. Tree mortality in drought-stressed mixed-conifer and ponderosa pine forests, Arizona, USA. *Forest Ecology and Management* 261: 162–68.

Gillis, J. 2011. The threats to a crucial canopy. *New York Times,* October 1, p. 1.

Rogstad, A., M. Crimmins, and G. Garfin. 2006. Climate change and wildfire impacts in the southwest forests and woodlands. Arizona Cooperative Extension, AZ1425, Tucson. 4 pp. http://cals.arizona.edu/pubs/natresources/az1425.pdf.

Veblen, T. T., T. Kitzberger, and J. Donnegan. 2000. Climatic and human influences on fire regimes in ponderosa pine forests in the Colorado Front Range. *Ecological Applications* 10 (4): 1178–95.

Waring, R. H., and B. E. Law. 2001. The ponderosa pine ecosystem and environmental stress: Past, present and future. *Tree Physiology* 21: 273–74.

Williams, A. P., C. D. Allen, C. I. Millar, T. W. Swetnam, J. Michaelsen, C. J. Still, and S. W. Leavitt. 2010. Forest responses to increasing aridity and warmth in the southwestern United States. *Proceedings of the National Academy of Sciences of the United States* 107 (50): 21289–94.

Dendrochronological Studies

Douglass, A. E. 1867–1962. Andrew Ellicott Douglass Papers. AZ 072. http://www.azarchivesonline.org/xtf/view?docId=ead/uoa/UAAZ072 .xml&doc.view=print;chunk.id=0.

———. 1920. Evidence of climatic effects in the annual rings of trees. *Ecology* 1 (1): 24–32.

———. 1929. The secret of the Southwest solved by talkative tree rings. *National Geographic* 56 (6): 736–70.

———. 1935. Dating Pueblo Bonito and Other Ruins of the Southwest. National Geographic Society, Contributed Technical Papers, Pueblo Bonito Series, no. 1. Washington, DC.

———. 1941. Crossdating in dendrochronology. *Journal of Forestry* 39: 825–31.

Grissino-Mayer, H. D. 2014. Gallery of Tree Rings 1. http://web.utk .edu/~grissino/treering-gallery1.htm.

Leverett, R. T. 2014. The big, the bigger, and the biggest: How we measure trees for championship status. Presented at The Southwest's Old Growth Forests. Conference, August 4–5, Fort Lewis College, Durango, CO.

McGraw, D. J. 2003. Andrew Ellicott Douglas and the giant sequoias in the founding of dendrochronology. *Tree-Ring Research* 59 (1): 21–27.

Reynolds, A. C., J. L. Betancourt, J. Quade, P. J. Patchett, J. S. Dean, and J. Stein. 2005. $^{87}Sr/^{86}Sr$ sourcing of ponderosa pine used in Anasazi great house construction at Chaco Canyon, New Mexico. *Journal of Archaeological Science* 32: 1061–75.

Schulman, E. 1940. *Tree Ring Bulletin* 6 (4). Tree Ring Society. University of Arizona, Tucson. 40 pp.

Speer, J. H. 2010. *Fundamentals of Tree Ring Research*. Tucson: University of Arizona Press. 368 pp.

Tree Ring Society website: http://www.treeringsociety.org/TRBTRR/ TRBTRR.htm.

van de Gevel, S., S. A. Finkelstein, V. Lenhartzen, D. W. Carr, M. Wienert, J. Duke, D. Achterhof, M. T. Kasson, L. Bissey, D. Kelly, and S. Maxwell. 2005. Field sampling and dendrochronological techniques in mixed conifer forests: A comparative study of Ponderosa

State Park and French Creek Road, central Idaho. Final report, Fifteenth Annual North American Dendroecological Fieldweek (NADEF). 17 pp. http://dendrolab.indstate.edu/nadef/reports/2005_vandegevel.pdf.

Fire and Ponderosa Pine Forests

Abella, S. R., W. W. Covington, P. Z. Fulé, L. B. Lentile, A. J. Sánchez Meador, and P. Morgan. 2007. Past, present, and future old growth in frequent-fire conifer forests of the western United States. *Ecology and Society* 12 (2): 16.

Anonymous. 2008. In a ponderosa pine forest, prescribed fires reduce the likelihood of scorched earth. Fire Science Brief 24:1–11. http://www.firescience.gov/projects/briefs/04–2–1–85_FSBrief24.pdf.

Arno, S. F., J. H. Scott, and M. G. Hartwell. 1995. Age class structure of old growth ponderosa pine/Douglas-fir stands and its relationship to fire history. Research Paper INT-RM-481 30. USDA Forest Service, Intermountain Research Station.

Bagne, K. E., and K. L. Purcell. 2009. Lessons learned from prescribed fire in ponderosa pine forests of the southern Sierra Nevada. In *Tundra to Tropics: Connecting Birds, Habitats and People*. Proceedings of Fourth International Partners in Flight Conference, pp. 679–90.

Blake, J. G. 1982. Influence of fires and logging on nonbreeding bird communities of ponderosa pine forests. *Journal of Wildlife Management* 46 (2): 405–15.

Brown, P. M. 2006. Climate effects on fire regimes and tree recruitment in Black Hills ponderosa pine forests. *Ecology* 87 (10): 2500–2510.

Brown, P. M., and C. H. Sieg. 1999. Historical variability in fire at the ponderosa pine–northern Great Plains prairie ecotone, southeastern Black Hills, South Dakota. *Ecoscience* 6 (4): 539–47.

Bryan, S. M., and B. Christie. 2011. Arizona fires rekindle debate over ponderosa pine forests. http://www.newsobserver.com/2011/06/10/1261524/arizona-fires-rekindle-debate.html.

Converse, S. J., G. C. White, and W. M. Block. 2006. Small mammal responses to thinning and wildfire in ponderosa pine–dominated forests of the southwestern United States. *Ecological Applications* 70 (6): 1711–22.

Covington, W. W., and M. M. Moore. 1994. Southwestern ponderosa forest structure—changes since Euro-American settlement. *Journal of Forestry* 92: 39–47.

Covington, W. W., and S. S. Sackett. 1984. The effects of prescribed burn in southwestern ponderosa pine on organic matter and nutrients in woody debris and forest floor. *Forest Science* 30 (1): 183–92.

———. 1986. Effect of periodic burning on soil nitrogen concentrations in ponderosa pine. *Soil Science Society of America Journal* 50 (2): 452–57.

Dieterich, J. H., and T. W. Swetnam. 1984. Dendrochronology of a fire-scarred ponderosa pine. *Forest Science* 30: 238–47.

Ffolliott, P. F., C. L. Stropki, H. Chen, and D. G. Neary. 2009. Observations of bird numbers and species following a historic wildfire in Arizona ponderosa pine forests. *Journal of the Arizona-Nevada Academy of Science* 41 (1): 16–23.

Gruell, G. E. 1985. Fire on the early western landscape: An annotated record of wildland fires 1776–1900. *Northwest Science* 59 (2): 97–107.

Guerin, E. 2012. Fire fights. *High Country News* 44 (16): 6–7, September 17.

Haasis, F. W. 1921. Relations between soil type and root form of western yellow pine seedlings. *Ecology* 2: 292–303.

Harris, G. R., and W. W. Covington. 1983. The effects of a prescribed fire on nutrient concentrations and standing crop of understory vegetation in ponderosa pine. *Canadian Journal of Forest Research* 13: 501–7.

Heyerdahl, E. K., and S. J. McKay. 2001. Condition of live fire-scarred ponderosa pine trees six years after removing partial cross sections. *Tree-Ring Research* 57 (2): 131–39.

Howard, Janet L. 2003. *Pinus ponderosa* var. *arizonica*. In *Fire Effects Information System*. USDA Forest Service, Rocky Mountain Research Station, Fire Sciences Laboratory. http://www.fs.fed.us/database/feis/.

Kyle, S. C., and W. M. Block. 2000. Effects of wildfire severity on small mammals in northern Arizona ponderosa pine forests. In *Fire and Forest Ecology: Innovative Silviculture and Vegetation Management,* ed. W. K. Moser and C. E. Moser, pp. 163–68. Tall Timbers Fire Ecology Conference Proceedings 21. Tall Timbers Research Station, Tallahassee, FL.

Moir, W. No date. Ponderosa pine fire ecology. In *Land Use History of North America, Colorado Plateau.* http://cpluhna.nau.edu/Biota/ponderosafire.htm.

Montoya, S. M., and B. Christie. 2011. Arizona fires rekindle debate over ponderosa pine forests. http://www.newsobserver.com/2011/06/10/1261524/arizona-fires-rekindle-debate.html.

Plummer, F. G. 1912. *Lightning in Relation to Forest Fires.* USDA Forest Service Bulletin 111. Washington, DC: U.S. Government Printing Office. 41 pp.

Rogstad, A. 2002. *Recovering from Wildfire: A Guide for Arizona's Forest Owners.* Tucson: Cooperative Extension, College of Agriculture and Life Sciences, University of Arizona. 15 pp.

Sackett, S. S. 1979. Natural fuel loading in ponderosa pine and mixed conifer forests of the Southwest. Research Paper RM-213. Fort Collins, CO: USDA Forest Service, Rocky Mountain Forest and Range Experiment Station. 11 pp.

Shinneman, D. J., and W. L. Baker. 1997. Nonequilibrium dynamics between catastrophic disturbances and old-growth forests in ponderosa pine landscapes of the Black Hills. *Conservation Biology* 11 (6): 1276–88.

Southern Methodist University. Ancient tree-ring records from southwest U.S. suggest today's megafires are truly unusual. *Sciencedaily,* Featured Research, May 16, 2012. http://www.sciencedaily.com/releases/2012/05/120516120304.htm.

Swetnam, T. W., and J. H. Dieterich. 1983. Fire history in the Gila Wilderness, New Mexico. http://www.ltrr.arizona.edu/~tswetnam/tws-pdf/gilawilderness.pdf.

Veblen, T. T., T. Kitzberger, and J. Donnegan. 2000. Climatic and human influences on fire regimes in ponderosa pine forests in the Colorado Front Range. *Ecological Applications* 10 (4): 1178–95.

Waldrop, T. A., and J. McLver. 2006. The national fire and fire surrogate study: Early results and future challenges. In *Proceedings of the 13th Biennial Southern Silvicultural Research Conference,* ed. K. F. Connor, pp. 526–30. General Technical Report SRS–92. Asheville, NC: USDA Forest Service, Southern Research Station.

Weaver, H. 1964. Fire and management problems in ponderosa pine. *Proceedings of the Annual Tall Timbers Fire Ecology Conference* 3: 60–79. Tallahassee, FL.

Wheelwright, J. 2006. Fire in the sky: Why America's ecological treasures sometimes just need to burn. *Discover* magazine (June).

Williams, G. W. 2001. References on the American Indian use of fire in ecosystems. USDA Forest Service, Washington, DC. http://www.wildlandfire.com/docs/biblio_indianfire.htm.

Williams, M. A., and W. L. Baker. 2012. Spatially extensive reconstructions show variable-severity fire and heterogeneous structure in historical western United States dry forests. In *Global Ecology and Biogeography.* doi: 10.1111/j.1466–8238.2011.00750.x.

Wilson, A. 2009. Overgrown pine forests still a danger. *Arizona Daily Sun,* January 22.

Foliage, Cones, Anatomy, and Physiology

Cable, D. R. 1958. Estimating surface area of ponderosa pine foliage in central Arizona. *Forest Science* 4: 45–49.

Callaham, R. Z., and J. W. Duffield. 1962. Heights of selected ponderosa pine seedlings during 20 years. In *Report from the Forest Genetics Workshop Proceedings,* pp. 10–13. Southern Forests Tree Improvement Commission Publication 22. Macon, GA.

Cooperrider, C. K. 1938. Recovery processes of ponderosa pine reproduction following injury to young annual growth. *Plant Physiology* 13: 5–27.

Dvorak, J., and J. Stokova. 1993. Structure of the needles in the early phases of development in *Pinus ponderosa* P. ex C. Lawson with special reference to plastids. *Annals of Botany* 72 (5): 423–31.

Fowells, H. A. 1941. The period of seasonal growth of ponderosa pine and associated species. *Journal of Forestry* 39: 601–7.

Harris, J. M. 1989. *Spiral Grain and Wave Phenomena in Wood Formation*. Berlin: Springer-Verlag. 214 pp.

Keen, F. P. 1940. Longevity of ponderosa pine. *Journal of Forestry* 38: 597–98.

Kittredge, J. 1944. Estimation of the amount of foliage of trees and shrubs. *Journal of Forestry* 42: 905–12.

Kraugh, H. 1934. Diameter growth of ponderosa pine as related to age and crown development. *Journal of Forestry* 32: 68–71.

Kubler, H. 1991. Function of spiral growth in trees. *Trees* 5: 125–35.

Larson, M. M., and G. H. Schubert. 1970. Cone crops of ponderosa pine in central Arizona including the influence of Abert squirrels. USDA Forest Service Research Paper RM-58. Fort Collins, CO: Rocky Mountain Forest and Range Experiment Station. 15 pp.

Maguire, W. P. 1956. Are ponderosa pine cone crops predictable? *Journal of Forestry* 54: 778–79.

Meyer, W. H. 1938. (Rev. ed. 1961). *Yield of Even-Aged Stands of Ponderosa Pines*. USDA Forest Service Technical Bulletin 630. 59 pp.

Minor, C. O. 1964. Site-index curves for young-growth ponderosa pine in northern Arizona. Research Note RM-37. USDA Forest Service, Rocky Mountain Forests and Range Experiment Station, Ft. Collins, CO. 8 pp.

Mitton, J. 2005. Spiral trees on windy ridges. Natural selections. *Daily Camera* (Boulder, CO), September 23.

Nicholls, J. W. P. 1965. The possible causes of spiral grain. In Proceedings of the Meeting Section 41. International Union of Forest Research Organizations (IUFRO), Melbourne, 1: 1–7.

Preston, R. D. 1950. Spiral structure and spiral growth: The development of spiral grain in conifers. *Forestry* 23 (1): 48–55.

Roeser, J., Jr. 1941. Some aspects of flower and cone production in ponderosa pine. *Journal of Forestry* 39: 534–36.

Schmid, J. M., S. A. Mata, and J. C. Mitchell. 1986. Number and condition of seeds in ponderosa pine cones in central Arizona. *Great Basin Naturalist* 46 (3): 449–51.

Siggins, H. W. 1933. Distribution and rate of fall of conifer seeds. *Journal of Agricultural Research* 47 (2): 119–28.

Skatter, S., and B. Kycera. 1998. The cause of the prevalent direction of the spiral grain patterns in conifers. *Trees* 12: 265–73.

Smith, R. H. 1977. *Monoterpenes of Ponderosa Pine Xylem Resin in Western United States*. General Technical Bulletin 1532. Berkeley, CA: USDA Forest Service, Pacific Southwest Forest and Range Experiment Station. 48 pp.

Sorensen, A. E. 1986. Seed dispersal by adhesion. *Annual Review of Ecology and Systematics* 17: 443–63.

Willits, S. 1994. "Black bark" ponderosa pine: Tree grade definition and value comparison with old-growth trees. *Western Journal of Applied Forestry* 9 (1): 8–13.

General References for Ponderosa Pine and Ponderosa Pine Forests

Abella, S. R. 2008. A unique old-growth ponderosa pine forest in northern Arizona. *Journal of the Arizona–Nevada Academy of Science* 40 (1): 1–11.

Anonymous. 1995. Ponderosa pine. Western Wood Products Association. http://www.wwpa.org.

———. 2005. Ponderosa pines for the ages. *Landmarks* (fall/winter): 1–8. Newsletter of the Five Valleys Land Trust and Rock Creek Trust. Missoula, MT.

———. 2010. Old growth pines provide window to healthy forest. *Inside NAU*, July 14. http://www4.nau/insidenau/bumps/2010/7_14_10/trees.html.

Arno, S. F., L. Ostlund, and R. E. Keane. 2008. Living artifacts—the ancient ponderosa pines of the West. *Magazine of Western History*, pp. 55–62.

Aumack, E. 2010. What tomorrow holds for Arizona ponderosa pine forests? *Grand Canyon Trust*. http://www.grandcanyontrust.org/news/2010/12/what-tomorrow-holds-for-arizona%E2%80%99s-ponderosa-pine-forests/.

Barrett, J. W., P. M. McDonald, F. Ranco Jr., and R. A. Ryker. 1980. Interior ponderosa pine. In *Forest Cover Types of the United States and Canada*, ed. F. H. Eyre, pp. 114–15. Washington, DC: Society of American Foresters. 148 pp.

Black, H. C. 1968. Fate of sown and naturally seeded coniferous seeds. In *Wildlife and Reforestation in the Pacific Northwest*. Proceedings of the Symposium, ed. H. C. Black. Corvallis: School of Forestry, Oregon State University.

California National Guard. 2008. California Guard rescues nation's largest ponderosa pine. http://www.army.mil/-news/2008/07/29/11317-california-guard-rescues-nations-largest-ponderosa-pine/.

Cooper, C. F. 1961. Patterns in ponderosa pine forests. *Ecology* 42 (3): 493–99.

Covington, W. W. 2110. Newest endangered species: Old growth pines. *Arizona Daily Sun*, April 15, p. A5.

Cowlin, R. W., P. A. Briegleb, and F. L. Moravets. 1942. *Forest Resources of the Ponderosa Pine Region of Washington and Oregon*. Miscellaneous Publication 490. Washington, DC: USDA Forest Service. 113 pp.

Critchfield, W. B., and E. L. Little Jr. 1966. *Geographic Distribution of the Pines of the World*. Miscellaneous Publication 991. Washington, DC: USDA Forest Service. 97 pp.

Dawson, C., A. Kratz, R. Garfias, T. Grant, K. Urban, and C. Spurrier. 1998. Wildflowers of ponderosa pine forests. http://www.fs.fed.us/wildflowers/kids/coloring/books/Wildflowers_of_Ponderosa_Pine_Forests.pdf.

DeGomez, T., and J. D. Bailey, eds. 1998. *Beyond the Ponderosa*. Flagstaff, AZ: Flagstaff Community Tree Board.

Eyre, F. H. 1980. *Forest Cover Types of the United States and Canada*. Washington, DC: Society of American Foresters. 148 pp.

Farjon, A. 2005. *Pines: Drawings and Description of the Genus* Pinus. 2nd ed. Boston: Brill. 235 pp.

———. 2008. *A Natural History of Conifers*. Portland, OR: Timber Press. 304 pp.

Fowells, H. A. 1965. *Silvics of Forest Trees of the United States*. Agriculture Handbook 271. Washington, DC: USDA Forest Service. 762 pp.

Fowells, H. A., and G. H. Schubert. 1956. Seed crops of forest trees in the pine region of California. USDA Technical Bulletin 1150. Washington, DC: U.S. Government Printing Office. 48 pp.

Fralish, J. S., and S. B. Franklin. 2002. *Taxonomy and Ecology of Woody Plants in North American Forests*. New York: John Wiley and Sons. 612 pp.

Frazio, J. R. 1992. Arbor Day Foundation Library of Trees: Ponderosa Pine. Arbor Day Foundation, Nebraska City, NE.

Griffith, C. 2005. *Dictionary of Botanical Epithets*. http://www.winternet.com/~chuckg/dictionary.html.

Hardin, J. W., D. J. Leopold, and F. M. White. 2001. *Harlow and Harrar's Textbook of Dendrology*. 9th ed. Dubuque, IA: McGraw-Hill. 534 pp.

Houk, R. 1993. The magnificent ponderosa. *Plateau* magazine. Museum of Northern Arizona, Flagstaff. 32 pp.

Huckaby, L. S., M. R. Kaufmann, P. J. Fornwalt, J. M. Stoker, and C. Dennis. 2003. *Field Guide to Old Ponderosa Pines in the Colorado Front Range*. General Technical Report RMRS-GTR-109. USDA Forest Service, Rocky Mountain Research Station. 43 pp.

Huckaby, L. S., M. R. Kaufmann, P. J. Fornwalt, J. M. Stoker, and C. Dennis. 2003. *Identification and Ecology of Old Ponderosa Pine Trees in the Colorado Front Range*. General Technical Report RMRS-GTR-110. USDA Forest Service, Rocky Mountain Research Station. 47 pp.

Kraker, D. 2009. Ponderosa pines: Rugged trees with a sweet smell. http://www.npr.org/2009/08/17/111803772/ponderosa-pines-rugged-trees-with-a-sweet-smell.

Lauria, F. 1996. Typification of *Pinus benthamiana* Hartw. (Pinaceae), a taxon deserving renewed botanical examination. *Annals Naturhistorisches Museum Wien* 98 (B Suppl.): 427–46.

Little, E. L. Jr. 1971. *Atlas of United States Trees*. Vol. 1: *Conifers and Important Hardwoods*. USDA Forest Service Miscellaneous

Publication 1146. Washington, DC: U.S. Government Printing Office. 9 pp., 200 maps.

McAvoy, D. 2008. World's oldest ponderosa pine found in Utah forest study. *Utah Forest News* 12 (1). Utah State University Cooperative Extension. 8 pp.

McManus, R. 2002. American roots. *Sierra* magazine (November/December).

Mills, E. A. 1914. *The Story of a Thousand-Year Pine*. Boston: Houghton Mifflin. 64 pp.

Mirov, N. T. 1967. *The Genus* Pinus. New York: Ronald Press. 602 pp.

Mirov, N. T., and J. Hasbrouck. 1976. *The Story of Pines*. Bloomington: Indiana University Press. 148 pp.

Muir, J. 1894. *The Mountains of California*. New York: New Century. 389 pp.

———. 1896. "The National Parks and Forest Reservations." Speech. Proceedings of the meeting of the Sierra Club held November 23, 1895. *Sierra Club Bulletin* 1 (7): 271–84.

Oliver, W. W., and R. A. Ryker. 1988. Ponderosa pine. http://www.na.fs .fed/spfo/pubs/silvics.

———. 1990. Ponderosa pine. In *Silvics of North America*, tech. coords. R. M. Burns and B. H. Honkala, vol. 1, pp. 413–24. Agricultural Handbook 654. Washington, DC: USDA Forest Service. 1383 pp.

Peattie, D. C. 1991. *A Natural History of Western Trees*. Boston: Houghton Mifflin. 751 pp.

States, J. S., and W. S. Gaud. 1995. Ecology of hypogeous fungi associated with ponderosa pine. I. Patterns of distribution and sporocarp production in some Arizona forests. *Mycologia* 89 (5): 712–21.

Sudworth, George B. 1917. *The Pine Trees of the Rocky Mountain Region*. USDA Bulletin 460. Washington, DC: U.S. Government Printing Office. 47 pp.

Swetnam, T. W., and P. M. Brown. 1992. Oldest known conifers in the southwestern United States: Temporal and special patterns of maximum age. In *Proceedings of a Workshop on Old-Growth Forests in the Rocky Mountains and Southwest: The Status of Our Knowledge*, tech. coords. M. R. Kaufmann, W. H. Moir, and R. L. Bassett, pp. 24–38. Portal, AZ.

Thomson, W. G. 1940. A growth rate classification of southwestern ponderosa pine. *Journal of Forestry* 38: 547–53.

University of Exeter, England. 2000. Catalogue of the Coniferaes on the university estate. http://www.exeter.ac.uk/conifers/index.htm.

Wang, Chi-wu. 1977. Genetics of ponderosa pine. https://archive.org/ stream/geneticsofponder34wang/geneticsofponder34wang_djvu.txt.

Wegner, R. G. 2010. Black Forest Regional Park Forestry and Noxious Weed Management Plan. A project by El Paso County Parks, El Paso County, Colorado. 159 pp.

Wennerberg, S. 2004. Plant guide: Ponderosa pine. USDA Natural Resources Conservation Service. National Plants Data Center, Baton Rouge, LA. 4 pp.

General References for This Book

Anonymous. No date. Ponderosa pine trees: Eastern Washington. http://www.bentler.us/eastern-washington/plants/trees/ponderosa.aspx.

———. 2014. Forest management—a historical perspective. http://www.fs.fed.us/forestmanagement/aboutus/histperspective.shtml.

Chase, J. S. 1911. *Cone-Bearing Trees of the California Mountains.* Chicago: C. McClurg. 99 pp.

Earle, C. J. 2013. The gymnosperm database. http://www.conifers.org.

Henry, M. 1953. *Brighty of the Grand Canyon.* Chicago: Rand McNally. 224 pp.

Integrated Taxonomic Information System. 2014. http://www.itis.gov.

Jackson, J. P. 1979. *The Biography of a Tree.* Middle Village, NY: Jonathan David Publishers. 199 pp.

Little, E. L., Jr. 1971. *Atlas of United States Trees.* Vol. 1: *Conifers and Important Hardwoods.* USDA Miscellaneous Publication 1146. 9 pp., 200 maps.

Mangum, R. K., and S. G. Mangum. 1993. *Flagstaff Historic Walk: A Stroll through Old Downtown.* Flagstaff, AZ: Hexagon Press. 64 pp.

Merrill-Maker, A. 2005. *Montana Almanac: The First, Best Source for Information about Big Sky Country.* 2nd ed. Guilford, CT: Globe Pequot Press. 384 pp.

Mills, E. A. 1909. *Wild Life of the Rockies.* Boston: Houghton Mifflin. 262 pp.

———. 1911. *The Spell of the Rockies.* Boston: Houghton Mifflin. 355 pp.

———. 1914. *The Story of a Thousand-Year Pine.* Boston: Houghton Mifflin. 64 pp.

Muir, J. 1894. *The Mountains of California.* New York: New Century. 389 pp.

———. 1938. *John of the Mountains: The Unpublished Journals of John Muir.* Madison: University of Wisconsin Press. 480 pp.

Muller, S. 2011. Pondering the ponderosas. *Arizona Daily Sun,* November 6, p. 10.

Murie, O. J. 1998. *A Field Guide to Animal Tracks.* Boston: Houghton Mifflin Harcourt. 375 pp.

Murphy, A. 1994. *Graced by Pines—the Ponderosa Pine in the American West.* Missoula, MT: Mountain Press. 119 pp.

National Forest Management Act of 1976. 16 U.S.C. 1600. http://www.fs.fed.us/emc/nfma/includes/NFMA1976.pdf.

Plant profile for *Pinus ponderosa* (ponderosa pine). USDA Natural Resources Conservation Service. http://plants.usda.gov/java/profile?symbol=PIPO.

Shapiro, A. 2008. SHOOT: Over 100 years of Forest Service photography. http://www.foresthistory.org/ASPNET/USFSPhotohist.pdf.

Sunset Crater Volcano National Monument. Geologic Resources Evaluation Report. National Park Service, U.S. Department of the Interior. http://www.nature.nps.gov/geology/inventory/publications/reports/sucr_gre_rpt_view.pdf.

Young, J. A., and C. G. Young. 1992. *Seeds of Woody Plants in North America*. Portland, OR: Dioscorides Press. 407 pp.

History of Ponderosa Pine and Ponderosa Pine Forests

Anonymous. 1932. Ponderosa pine now official. *Journal of Forestry* 30: 510.

Bergon, F. 1989. Edited version of *The Journal of Lewis and Clark*. New York: Viking Penguin. 505 pp.

Betancourt, J. L. 1990. Late Quaternary biogeography of the Colorado Plateau. In *Packrat Middens: The Last 40,000 Years of Biotic Change,* ed. J. L. Betancourt, T. R. Van Devender, and P. S. Martin, pp. 259–92. Tucson: University of Arizona Press. 468 pp.

Cooper, C. F. 1960. Changes in Vegetation, Structure, and Growth of Southwestern Pine Forests since White Settlement. *Ecological Monographs* 30 (2). 164 pp.

Douglas, D. 1914. *Journal Kept by David Douglas during His Travels in North America, 1821–1827*. Published under the direction of the Royal Horticultural Society. London: William Wesley and Son. 382 pp.

Dutton, C. E. 1887. *Physical Geology of the Grand Canyon District*. In Second Annual Report of the U.S. Geological Survey, pp. 49–166. Washington, DC: U.S. Government Printing Office.

Keen, F. Paul. Oral history interview. Forest History Society. USDA Forest Service. http://www.foresthistory.org/research/Keen_Ohi_Final.pdf.

LaBau, V. J., J. T. Bones, N. P. Kingsley, H. G. Lund, and W. B. Smith. 2007. *A History of the Forest Survey in the United States 1830–2004*. USDA Forest Service FS-877. 81 pp.

Lauria, F. 1996. The identity of "Pinus ponderosae" Douglas ex C. Lawson (Pinaceae). *Linzer Biologische Beitraege* 28 (2): 999–1052.

Lewis, J. G. 2006. *The Forest Service and the Greatest Good: A Centennial History*. Washington, DC: Forest Service Society. 290 pp.

Lewis, M., W. Clark, and Members of the Corps of Discovery. September 4, 1806. In *The Journals of the Lewis and Clark Expedition*, ed. G. Moulton. Lincoln: University of Nebraska Press, 2002. Retrieved October 1, 2005, from http://lewisandclarkjournals.unl.edu/journals.php?id=1806–09–04.

Merriam, C. H., and L. Stejneger. 1890. *Results of a Biological Survey of the San Francisco Mountain Region and the Desert of the Little Colorado, Arizona*. North American Fauna 3. Washington, DC: U.S. Department of Agriculture, Division of Ornithology and Mammalia. 136 pp.

Nisbet, J. 2009. *The Collector: David Douglas and the Natural History of the Northwest.* Seattle: Sasquatch Books. 288 pp.

Olberding, S. D., and M. M. Moore, tech coords. 2008. *Forest Valley Experimental Forest—A Century of Research, 1908–2008.* Conference Proceedings RMRS-P-55. Fort Collins, CO: USDA Forest Service, Rocky Mountain Research Station. 282 pp.

Palmer, A. W. 1911. *The Mountain Trail and Its Message.* Boston: Pilgrim Press. 48 pp.

Patton, D. R. 2008. The Fort Valley Experimental Forest, ponderosa pine, and wildlife habitat research. In *Fort Valley Experimental Forest, a Century of Research 1908–2008,* tech. coords. S. D. Olberding and M. M. Moore. U.S. Forest Service Proceedings RMRS-P-53. Fort Collins, CO: USDA Forest Service, Rocky Mountain Research Station. 408 pp.

Railroad logging on the Coconino and Kaibab National Forests, 1887–1966. National Register of Historic Places. Multiple Property Documentation Form. http://pdfhost.focus.nps.gov/docs/NRHP/Text/64500041.pdf.

Raish, C., W. Yong, and J. Marzluff. 1997. Contemporary human use of southwestern ponderosa pine forests. In *Songbird Ecology in Southwestern Ponderosa Pine Forests: A Literature Review.* USDA Forest Service General Technical Report RM-GTR-292, tech. eds. W. M. Block and D. M. Finch. 14 pp.

Scurlock, D., and D. M. Finch. 1997. Historical review in songbird status and roles. In *Songbird Ecology in Southwestern Ponderosa Pine Forests: A Literature Review.* USDA Forest Service General Technical Report RM-GTR-292, tech. eds. W. M. Block and D. M. Finch. 25 pp.

Steen, H. K. 2004. *The U.S. Forest Service: A History.* Seattle: University of Washington Press. 432 pp.

Warner, T. J. 1995. *The Dominguez-Escalante Journal. Their Expedition through Colorado, Utah, Arizona, and New Mexico in 1776.* Translated by F. A. Chavez. Salt Lake City: University of Utah Press. 153 pp.

White, C. A. 2008. Durability of bearing trees. Bureau of Land Management. http://www.nevadasurveyor.com/bearing_trees/.

Insects, Fungi, and Infectious Diseases of Ponderosa Pine Trees

Amman, G. D., M. D. McGregor, and R. E. Dolph Jr. 1990. *Mountain Pine Beetle.* Forest Insect and Disease Leaflet 2. USDA Forest Service. http://www.barkbeetles.org/mountain/fid12.htm.

Anonymous. 2007. Western pine beetle (*Dendroctonus brevicomis*). Forest Health Note. Oregon Department of Forestry. Salem. 2 pp.

Bega, R. V., and R. F. Scharpf. 1993. *Diseases of Pacific Coast Conifers.* Agriculture Handbook 521, tech. coord. R. F. Scharpf. Albany, CA: USDA Forest Service, Pacific Southwest Research Station. 199 pp.

Bennett, M. No date. Why are my trees dying? And what can I do about it? Southern Oregon Forestry and Extension Center Note 3. http://extension.oregonstate.edu/sorec/sick-tree-information# PONDEROSA PINE.

Blue stain. USDA Forest Service, Forest Products Laboratory. http://www.fpl.fs.fed.us/documnts/techline/blue-stain.pdf.

Blue stain fungus. In *Field Guide to Insects and Diseases of Arizona and New Mexico Forests.* USDA Forest Service. http://www.fs.fed.us/r3/resources/health/field-guide/sds/bluestain.shtml.

Cole, W. F. 1966. Effects of pine butterfly defoliation on ponderosa pine in southern Idaho. USDA Forest Service Research Note INT-46. Ogden, UT: Intermountain Forest and Range Experiment Station. 7 pp.

Conklin, D. A., and M. L. Fairweather. 2010. *Dwarf Mistletoes and Their Management in the Southwest.* R-3-FH-10–01. Berkeley, CA: USDA Forest Service, Southwestern Region. 23 pp.

Edmonds, G. F. Jr., and D. N. Alstad. 1978. Coevolution in insect herbivores and conifers. *Science* 199: 941–45.

Evenden, J. C. 1940. Effects of defoliation by the pine butterfly upon ponderosa pine. *Journal of Forestry* 38: 949–55.

Gillis, J. 2011. The threats to a crucial canopy. *New York Times,* October 1, p. 1.

Hawksworth, F. G. 1977. *The 6-Class Dwarf Mistletoe Rating System.* General Technical Report RM-48. Fort Collins, CO: USDA Forest Service, Rocky Mountain Forest and Range Experiment Station. 7 pp.

Hawksworth, F. G., and D. Wiens. 1996. *Dwarf Mistletoes: Biology, Pathology, and Systematics.* Agricultural Handbook 709 (supersedes AH-401). Fort Collins, CO: USDA Rocky Mountain Forest and Range Experiment Station. 410 pp.

Hepting, G. H. 1971. *Diseases of Forest and Shade Trees of the United States.* Agriculture Handbook 386. USDA Forest Service. Washington, DC: U.S. Government Printing Office. 658 pp.

Keen, F. P. 1943. Ponderosa pine tree classes redefined. *Journal of Forestry* 41 (4): 249–53.

———. 1955. The rate of natural falling of beetle-killed ponderosa pine snags. *Journal of Forestry* 53 (10): 720–23.

———. 1976. *The western pine beetle.* USDA Forest Service, Forest Pest Leaflet 1. 4 pp.

Kulman, H. M. 1971. Effects of insect defoliation on growth and mortality of trees. *Annual Review of Entomology* 16: 289–324.

Larsson, S., R. Oren, R. H. Waring, and J. W. Barrett. 1983. Attacks of mountain pine beetle as related to tree vigor of ponderosa pine. *Forest Science* 29 (2): 395–402.

Lekson, S. H. 2007. *The Architecture of Chaco Canyon, New Mexico.* Chaco Canyon Series. Salt Lake City: University of Utah Press. 296 pp.

Lundquist, J. E., and R. M. Reich. 2006. Tree diseases, canopy structure, and bird distributions in ponderosa pine forests. *Journal of Sustainable Forestry* 23 (2): 17–45.

Miller, J. M., and F. P. Keen. 1960. *Biology and Control of the Western Pine Beetle.* Publication 800. USDA Forest Service. MBC. 381 pp.

Miller, P. R. 1993. *Diseases of Pacific Coast Conifers.* Agriculture Handbook 521, tech. coord. R. F. Scharpf. Albany, CA: USDA Forest Service, Pacific Southwest Research Station. 199 pp.

Mooney, K. A. 2007. Tritrophic effects of birds and ants on a canopy food web, tree growth, and phytochemistry. *Ecology* 88 (8): 2005–14.

Nicholls, T. H., F. G. Hawksworth, and L. M. Merrill. 1984. Animal vectors of dwarf mistletoe, with special reference to *Arceuthobium americanum* on lodgepole pine. In *Biology of Dwarf Mistletoes: Proceedings of the Symposium, August 8, 1984, Colorado State University, Fort Collins,* tech. coords. F. G. Hawksworth and R. F. Scharp, pp. 102–10. General Technical Report RM-111. Fort Collins, CO: USDA Forest Service, Rocky Mountain Forest and Range Experiment Station.

Ponderosa pine seedworm. In *Field Guide to Insects and Diseases of Arizona and New Mexico Forests.* USDA Forest Service. http://www.fs.fed.us/r3/resources/health/field-guide/csi/ponderosa.shtml.

Randall, C. B. 2010. Management guide for western pine beetle. USDA Forest Service. 7 pp. http://www.fs.usda.gov/Internet/FSE_DOCUMENTS/stelprdb5188577.pdf.

Schmid, J. M., and D. D. Bennett. 1988. *The North Kaibab Pandora Moth Outbreak, 1978–1984.* General Technical Report RM-153. Fort Collins, CO: USDA Forest Service, Rocky Mountain Forest and Range Experimental Station. 18 pp.

Schmid, J. M., S. A. Mata, and W. F. McCambridge. 1985. Natural falling of beetle-killed ponderosa pine. USDA Forest Service Research Note RM-454. Fort Collins, CO: Rocky Mountain Forest and Range Experiment Station. 4 pp.

Schmid, J. M., J. C. Mitchell, K. D. Carlin, and M. R. Wagner. 1984. Insect damage, cone dimensions, and seed production in crown levels of ponderosa pine. *Great Basin Naturalist* 44 (4): 575–78.

Smith, C. C., and R. P. Balda. 1979. Competition among insects, birds, and mammals for conifer seeds. *American Zoologist* 19: 1065–83.

Smith, R. S., Jr., and R. F. Scharpf. 1993. *Diseases of Pacific Coast Conifers.* Agriculture Handbook 521, tech. coord. R. F. Scharpf. Albany, CA: USDA Forest Service, Pacific Southwest Research Station. 199 pp.

Stevens, R. E. *Pine reproduction weevil.* 1971. USDA Forest Service, Forest Pest Leaflet 15. 6 pp.

Velush, L. 1996. Parasitic plant threatens health of old ponderosas. *Arizona Daily Sun,* September 17.

Western pine shoot borer. 2007. Forest Health Note. Oregon Department of Forestry. http://www.oregon.gov/odf/privateforests/docs/fh/westernpine shootborer.pdf

Lightning

Abiotic stem damage—injury or damage from non-living agents. USDA Forest Service. http://www.fs.usda.gov/Internet/FSE_DOCUMENTS/stelprdb5353711.pdf.

Clatterbuck, W. K., D. S. Vandergriff, and K. D. Coder. Understanding lightning and associated tree damage. Tree Care Kit. AgriLIFE Extension, Texas A&M System. http://essmextension.tamu.edu/treecarekit/index.php/after-the-storm/tree-damage-and-hazard-assessment/understanding-lightning-and-associated-tree-damage/.

DeRosa, E. W. 1983. Lightning and trees. *Journal of Arboriculture* 9 (2): 51–53.

Smith, W. H. 1970. *Tree Pathology: A Short Introduction.* New York: Academic Press. 309 pp.

Mammals of the Ponderosa Pine Forests

Allred, S. 2011. *The Natural History of Tassel-Eared Squirrels.* Albuquerque: University of New Mexico Press. 320 pp.

Allred, W. S., and W. S. Gaud. 1993. Green foliage losses from ponderosa pines induced by Abert squirrels and snowstorms: A comparison. *Western Journal of Applied Forestry* 8: 16–18.

———. 1994a. Characteristics of ponderosa pines and Abert squirrel herbivory. *Southwestern Naturalist* 39: 89–90.

———. 1994b. Effects of Abert squirrel herbivory on foliage and nitrogen losses in ponderosa pine. *Southwestern Naturalist* 39: 350–53.

Allred, W. S., W. S. Gaud, and J. S. States. 1994. Effects of herbivory by Abert squirrels (*Sciurus aberti*) on cone crops of ponderosa pine. *Journal of Mammalogy* 75: 700–703.

Chambers, C. L. 2002. *Forest Management and the Dead Wood Resource in Ponderosa Pine Forests: Effects on Small Mammals.* General Technical Report PSW-GTR-181. USDA Forest Service.

Chambers, C. L., V. Alm, M. S. Siders, and M. J. Rabe. 2002. Use of artificial roosts by forest-dwelling bats in northern Arizona. *Wildlife Society Bulletin* 30 (4): 1085–91.

Converse, S. J., B. G. Dickson, G. C. White, and W. M. Block 2004. Estimating small mammal abundance on fuels treatment units in southwestern ponderosa pine forests. In *The Colorado Plateau: Cultural, Biological, and Physical Research,* ed. C. van Riper III and K. L. Cole, pp. 113–20. Tucson: University of Arizona Press.

Converse, S. J., G. C. White, and W. M. Block. 2006. Small mammal responses to thinning and wildfire in ponderosa pine–dominated forests of the southwestern United States. *Ecological Applications* 70 (6): 1711–22.

Curtis, J. D. 1948. Animals that eat ponderosa pine seed. *Journal of Wildlife Management* 12 (3): 327–28.

Curtis, J. D., and A. K. Wilson. 1953. Porcupine feeding on ponderosa pine in central Idaho. *Journal of Forestry* 51: 339–41.

Evans, J. 1988. Animal damage and its control in ponderosa pine forests. In *Ponderosa Pine: The Species and Its Management,* ed. D. M. Baumgartner and J. E. Lotan. Proceedings of the symposium, September 29–October 1, 1987, Spokane, WA.

Fiehler, C. M. 2007. Dispersal of ponderosa pine (*Pinus ponderosa*) seeds by shadow chipmunks (*Tamias senex*) in a managed forest. Master's thesis. Humboldt State University, Arcata, CA. 35 pp.

Grinnell, J., and T. I. Storer. 1924. *Animal Life in the Yosemite: An Account of the Mammals, Birds, Reptiles, and Amphibians in a Cross Section of the Sierra Nevada.* Berkeley: University of California Press. 752 pp.

Heidmann, L. J. 1972. An initial assessment of mammal damage in the forests of the Southwest. USDA Forest Service Research Note RM-219. 7 pp.

Hoovens, E. F. 1969. Animal damage to seed and seedlings. In *Proceedings of Symposium—Regeneration of Ponderosa Pine,* ed. R. K. Herman, paper 681. Oregon State University School of Forestry.

Keith, J. O. 1965. The Abert squirrel and its dependence on ponderosa pine. *Ecology* 46: 150–63.

Kyle, S. C., and W. M. Block. 2000. Effects of wildfire severity on small mammals in northern Arizona ponderosa pine forests. In *Fire and Forest Ecology: Innovative Silviculture and Vegetation Management,* ed. W. K. Moser and C. E. Moser, pp. 163–68. Tall Timbers Fire Ecology Conference Proceedings 21. Tall Timbers Research Station, Tallahassee, FL.

Larson, M. M., and G. H. Schubert. 1970. Cone crops of ponderosa pine in central Arizona including the influence of Abert squirrels. USDA Forest Service Research Paper RM-58. Fort Collins, CO: Rocky Mountain Forest and Range Experiment Station. 15 pp.

Loucks, D. M., H. C. Black, M. L. Roush, and S. R. Radosevich. 1990. *Assessment and Management of Animal Damage in Pacific Northwest Forests: An Annotated Bibliography.* General Technical Report PNW-GTR-262. USDA Forest Service, Pacific Northwest Research Station. 376 pp.

Merriam, C. H., and L. Stejneger. 1890. *Results of a Biological Survey of the San Francisco Mountain Region and the Desert of the Little Colorado, Arizona.* North American Fauna 3. Washington, DC: U.S. Department of Agriculture, Division of Ornithology and Mammalia. 136 pp.

Moir, W. H., B. Geils, M. A. Benoit, and D. Scurlock. 1997. Ecology of southwestern ponderosa pine forests. In *Songbird Ecology in*

Southwestern Ponderosa Pine Forests: A Literature Review. USDA Forest Service General Technical Report RM-GTR-292, tech. eds. W. M. Block and D. M. Finch. 27 pp.

Patton, D. R. 1974. Characteristics of ponderosa pine stands selected by Abert's squirrels for cover. Ph.D. diss., University of Arizona, Tucson. 40 pp.

———. 1977. Managing southwestern ponderosa pine for the Abert squirrel. *Journal of Forestry* 75: 264–67.

———. 1984. A model to evaluate Abert squirrel habitat in uneven-aged ponderosa pine. *Wildlife Society Bulletin* 12: 408–14.

———. 1989. Wildlife habitat concerns: Moderator's comments. In *Multiresource Management of Ponderosa Pine Forests.* Proceedings, ed. A. Tecle, W. W. Covington, and R. H. Hamre, p. 130. General Technical Report RM-185. USDA Forest Service. 282 pp.

———. 1997. *Wildlife Habitat Relationships in Forested Ecosystems.* 2nd ed. Portland, OR: Timber Press. 502 pp.

Patton, D. R., and W. Green. 1970. Abert's squirrels prefer mature ponderosa pine. USDA Forest Service Research Note RM-169, Fort Collins, CO: Rocky Mountain Forest and Range Experiment Station. 3 pp.

Pike, G. W. 1934. Girdling of ponderosa pine by squirrels. *Journal of Forestry* 32: 98–99.

Rabe, M. J., T. E. Morrell, H. Green, J. C. deVos Jr., and C. R. Miller. 1998. Characteristics of ponderosa pine snag roosts used by reproductive bats in northern Arizona. *Journal of Wildlife Management* 62 (2): 612–21.

Schubert, G. H. 1953. Ponderosa pine cone cutting by squirrels. *Journal of Forestry* 51: 202.

Skinner, T. H., and J. O. Klemmedson. 1978. Abert squirrels influence nutrient transfer through litterfall in a ponderosa pine forest. USDA Forest Service Research Note RM-353. Fort Collins, CO: Rocky Mountain Research Station. 8 pp.

Smith, C. C., and R. P. Balda. 1979. Competition among insects, birds, and mammals for conifer seeds. *American Zoologist* 19: 1065–83.

Smith, C. F., and S. E. Aldous. 1947. The influence of mammals and birds in retarding artificial and natural reseeding of coniferous forests in the United States. *Journal of Forestry* 45: 361–69.

Smith, T. G., and C. C. Maguire. 2004. Small-mammal relationships with down wood and antelope bitterbrush in ponderosa pine forests of Central Oregon. *Forest Science* 50 (5): 711–28.

Tevis, L., Jr. 1953. Effects of vertebrate animals on seed crops of sugar pine. *Journal of Wildlife Management* 17 (2): 128–31.

Vavra, M., K. Walbunger, and T. DelCurto. 2005. *Ungulate Ecology of Ponderosa Pine Ecosystems in the Northwest.* USDA Forest Service General Technical Report PSW GTR-198. 14 pp.

Waters, J. R., and C. J. Zabel. 1998. Abundance of small mammals in fir forests in northeastern California. *Journal of Mammalogy* 79 (4): 1244–53.

Mushrooms and Truffles in Ponderosa Pine Forests

States, J. S. 1990. *Mushrooms and Truffles of the Southwest*. Tucson: University of Arizona Press. 234 pp.

Plant Associations of Ponderosa Pine Forests

Biotic communities of the Colorado Plateau-Ponderosa pine forest. No date. http://cpluhna.nau.edu/Biota/ponderosa_forest.htm.

Moir, W. H., B. Geils, M. A. Benoit, and D. Scurlock. 1997. Ecology of southwestern ponderosa pine forests. In *Songbird Ecology in Southwestern Ponderosa Pine Forests: A Literature Review*. USDA Forest Service General Technical Report RM-GTR-292, tech. eds. W. M. Block and D. M. Finch. 27 pp.

Ponderosa Pine Ecology

Allen, C. D., M. Savage, D. A. Falk, K. F. Suckling, T. W. Swetnam, T. Schulke, P. B. Stacey, P. Morgan, M. Hoffman, and J. T. Klingel. 2002. Ecological restoration of southwestern ponderosa pine ecosystem: A broad perspective. *Ecological Applications* 12 (5): 1418–33.

Biotic communities of the Colorado Plateau. In *Land Use History of North America, Colorado Plateau*. http://cpluhna.nau.edu/Biota/ponderosa_forest.htm.

Brown, D. E. 1994. *Biotic Communities: Southwestern United States and Northwestern Mexico*. Salt Lake City: University of Utah Press. 342 pp.

Brown, D. E., and C. H. Lowe. 1980. *Biotic Communities of the Southwest*. General Technical Report RM–78. Fort Collins, CO: USDA Forest Service, Rocky Mountain Range and Experiment Station.

Brown, D. E., C. H. Lowe, and C. P. Pase. 1979. A digitized classification system for the biotic communities of North America, with community (series) and association examples for the Southwest. *Journal of the Arizona-Nevada Academy of Science* 14 (1): 1–16. Supplement 1. http://www.jstor.org/stable/40025041.

Coconino National Forest. USDA Forest Service website. http://www.fs.fed.us/r3/coconino/nepa/flea2_health.html.

Daubenmire, R. F. 1938. Merriam's life zones of North America. *Quarterly Review of Biology* 13 (3): 327–32.

Eversman, S. 1982. Epiphytic lichens of ponderosa pine forest in southeastern Montana. *Bryologist* 85 (2): 204–13.

Friederici, P. 2003. *Ecological Restoration of Southwestern Ponderosa Pine Forests*. Washington, DC: Island Press. 584 pp.

Huckaby, L. S., M. R. Kaufmann, P. J. Fornwalt, J. M. Stoker, and C. Dennis. 2003. *Identification and Ecology of Old Ponderosa Pine Trees in the Colorado Front Range*. General Technical Report RMRS-GTR-110. Rocky Mountain Research Station. 47 pp.

Hungate, B. A., S. C. Hart, P. C. Selmants, S. I. Boyle, and C. A. Gehring. 2007. Soil responses to management, increased precipitation, and added nitrogen in ponderosa pine forests. *Ecological Applications* 5: 1352–65.

Merriam, C. H., and L. Stejneger. 1890. *Results of a Biological Survey of the San Francisco Mountain Region and the Desert of the Little Colorado, Arizona.* North American Fauna 3. Washington, DC: U.S. Department of Agriculture, Division of Ornithology and Mammalia. 136 pp.

Moir, W. H., B. Geils, M. A. Benoit, and D. Scurlock. 1997. Ecology of southwestern ponderosa pine forests. In *Songbird Ecology in Southwestern Ponderosa Pine Forests: A Literature Review.* USDA Forest Service General Technical Report RM-GTR-292, tech. eds. W. M. Block and D. M. Finch, 27 pp.

Patton, D. R. 1997. *Wildlife Habitat Relationships in Forested Ecosystems.* 2nd ed. Portland, OR: Timber Press. 502 pp.

Richardson, D. M., and P. W. Rundel. 1998. *Ecology and Biogeography of* Pinus, ed. D. M. Richardson, Cambridge, U.K.: Cambridge University Press. 527 pp.

Thomas, J. W. 1999. Dead wood: From forester's bane to environmental boon. In *Proceedings of the Symposium on the Ecology and Management of Dead Wood in Western Forests,* tech. coords. W. F. Laudenslayer Jr., P. J. Shea, B. E. Valentine, C. P. Weatherspoon, and T. E. Lisle, pp. 3–10. November 2–4, Reno, Nevada.

Ponderosa Pine Forest Management

Covington, W., and P. K. Wagner, tech. coords. 1996. *Proceedings of the Conference on Adaptive Ecosystem Restoration and Management: Restoration of Cordilleran Conifer Landscapes of North America.* General Technical Report RM-GTR-278. USDA Forest Service. 91 pp.

Fule, P. Z., W. W. Covington, and M. M. Moore. 1997. Determining reference conditions for ecosystem management of southwestern ponderosa pine forests. *Ecological Applications* 7: 895–908.

Hatz, R. 2007. *Managing Ponderosa Pine Woodlands for Fish and Wildlife.* Woodland Fish and Wildlife Project Publication. Pullman: Washington State University Extension Publishing and Printing. 12 pp.

Hunter, M. L. 1990. *Wildlife, Forests, and Forestry: Principles of Managing Forests for Biological Diversity.* Englewood Cliffs, NJ: Prentice-Hall. 370 pp.

Larson, M. M., and G. H. Schubert. 1970. Cone crops of ponderosa pine in central Arizona including the influence of Abert squirrels. Research Paper RM-58. Fort Collins, CO: USDA Forest Service, Rocky Mountain Forest and Range Experiment Station. 15 pp.

Loucks, D. M., H. C. Black, M. L. Roush, and S. R. Radosevich. 1990. *Assessment and Management of Animal Damage in Pacific Northwest Forests: An Annotated Bibliography.* General Technical Report

PNW-GTR-262. USDA Forest Service, Pacific Northwest Research Station. 376 pp.

Patton, D. R. 1977. Managing southwestern ponderosa pine for the Abert squirrel. *Journal of Forestry* 75: 264–67.

———. 1984. A model to evaluate Abert squirrel habitat in uneven-aged ponderosa pine. *Wildlife Society Bulletin* 12: 408–14.

———. 1989. Wildlife habitat concerns: Moderator's comments. In *Multiresource Management of Ponderosa Pine Forests*, Proceedings, ed. A. Tecle, W. W. Covington, and R. H. Hamre, p. 130. USDA Forest Service General Technical Report RM-185. 282 pp.

———. 1997. *Wildlife Habitat Relationships in Forested Ecosystems.* 2nd ed. Portland, OR: Timber Press. 502 pp.

Pearson, G. A. 1950. *Management of Ponderosa Pine in the Southwest.* Agriculture Monograph 6. USDA Forest Service. 218 pp.

Thomas, J. W. 1979. *Wildlife Habitats in Managed Forests: The Blue Mountains of Oregon and Washington.* Agriculture Handbook 553. USDA Forest Service. 512 pp.

———. 1999. Dead wood: From forester's bane to environmental boon. In *Proceedings of the Symposium on the Ecology and Management of Dead Wood in Western Forests*, tech. coords. W. F. Laudenslayer Jr., P. J. Shea, B. E. Valentine, C. P. Weatherspoon, and T. E. Lisle, pp. 3–10. November 2–4, Reno, Nevada.

Silviculture in Ponderosa Pine Forests

Barrett, S. W., and S. F. Arno. 1988. *Increment-Borer Methods for Determining Fire History in Coniferous Forests.* General Technical Report INT-244. USDA Forest Service, Intermountain Research Station. 20 pp.

Briegleb, P. A. 1943. Growth of ponderosa pine by Keen tree class. Forest Research Note 32. Pacific Northwest Forest Experiment Station, Portland, OR. 16 pp. http://www.fs.fed.us/pnw/pubs/journals/pnw_os_rn-032.pdf.

Callaham, R. Z., and J. W. Duffield. 1962. Heights of selected ponderosa pine seedlings during 20 years. In *Report from the Forest Genetics Workshop Proceedings*, pp. 10–13. Southern Forests Tree Improvement Commission Publication 22. Macon, GA.

Clapp, E. H. 1912. Silvicultural systems for western yellow pine. *Proceedings of the Society of American Foresters* 7: 168–76.

Fiske, J., and J. Tappeiner. 2005. *An Overview of Key Silvicultural Information for Ponderosa Pine.* Technical Report PSW-GTR-198. USDA Forest Service. 15 pp.

Fowells, H. A. 1956. Are ponderosa pine cone crops predictable? *Journal of Forestry* 54: 778–79.

Keen, F. P. 1943. Ponderosa pine tree classes redefined. *Journal of Forestry* 41 (4): 249–53.

Maeglin, R. R. 1979. *Increment Cores: How to Collect, Handle, and Use Them*. General Technical Report FPL 25. USDA Forest Service, Forest Products Laboratory. 21 pp.

Minor, C. O. 1964. Site-index curves for young-growth ponderosa pine in northern Arizona. U.S. Forest Service Research Note RM-37. Fort Collins, CO: Rocky Mountain Forests and Range Experiment Station. 8 pp.

Schubert, G. H. 1969. Ponderosa pine regeneration problems in the Southwest. In *Regeneration of Ponderosa Pine Symposium*, ed. R. K. Hermann, paper 681. Corvallis: Oregon State University School of Forestry.

———. 1974. Silviculture of the southwestern ponderosa pine: The status of our knowledge. USDA Forest Service Research Paper RM-123. 71 pp.

Timber harvesting methods. 2007. Maine Forestry. http://maineforestry .net/Forestry%20Items/timber_hvt_methods.htm.

Trails of the Past: Historical overview of the Flathead National Forest, Montana 1800–1960. No date. Forest History Society. USDA Forest Service. http://www.foresthistory.org/ASPNET/Publications/ region/1/flathead/chap10.htm.

Snags in Ponderosa Pine Forests

Bottorff, J. 2009. Snags, coarse woody debris, and wildlife. Washington State Department of Natural Resources. 5 pp. http://snohomish.wsu .edu/forestry/documents/SNAGS.pdf.

Chambers, C. L., and J. N. Mast. 2005. Ponderosa pine snag dynamics and cavity excavation following wildfire in northern Arizona. *Forest Ecology and Management* 216: 227–40.

Ganey, J. L., and S. C. Vojta. 2004. Characteristics of snags containing excavated cavities in northern Arizona mixed-conifer and ponderosa pine forests. *Forest Ecology and Management* 199: 323–32.

Keen, F. P. 1955. The rate of natural falling of beetle-killed ponderosa pine snags. *Journal of Forestry* 53 (10): 720–23.

Neitro, W. A., R. W. Mannan, D. Taylor, V. W. Binkley, B. G. Marcot, F. F. Wagner, and S. P. Cline. Snags (wildlife trees). http://www.fs.fed .us/r6/nr/wildlife/animalinn/hab_wlsnag.htm.

Nickens, T. E. 2002. Snags and widowmakers. Wild things. *Backpacker* 30 (204): 29.

Schmid, J. M., S. A. Mata, and W. F. McCambridge. 1985. Natural falling of beetle-killed ponderosa pine. USDA Forest Service Research Note RM-454. Fort Collins, CO: Rocky Mountain Forest and Range Experiment Station. 4 pp.

Waskiewicz, J. D., P. Z. Fule, and P. Beier. 2007. Comparing classification systems for ponderosa pine snags in northern Arizona. *Western Journal of Applied Forestry* 22 (4): 233–40.

Spiral Growth

Kuber, H. 1991. Function of spiral grain in trees. *Trees* 5: 125–35.

Northcott, P. L. 1957. Is spiral grain the normal growth pattern. *Forest Chronicle* 33 (4): 335–52.

Uses of Ponderosa Pines

Joye, N. M. Jr., A. T. Proveaux, R. V. Lawrence, and R. L. Barger. 1969. Naval stores products from ponderosa pine stumps. *Industrial and Engineering Chemistry Product Research Development* 8 (3): 297–99.

Kurth, E. F., and J. K. Hubbard. 1951. Extractives from ponderosa pine bark. *Industrial and Engineering Chemistry* 43 (4): 896–900.

Moerman, D. E. 1998. *Native American Ethnobotany*. Portland, OR: Timber Press. 927 pp.

Ostlund, L., L. Ahlberg, O. Zackrisson, I. Bergman, and S. Arno. 2009. Bark-peeling, food stress, and tree spirits—the use of pine inner bark for food in Scandinavia and North America. *Journal of Ethnobiology* 29 (1): 94–112.

Ponderosa pine. Lewis and Clark Historic Trail. U.S. Department of the Interior, National Park Service. http://www.nps.gov/lecl/naturescience/ponderosa-pine.htm.

Prizer, T. No date. Catfaces: Totems of Georgia's turpentiners. http://www.dailyyonder.com/totems-georgias-lost-turpentine-industry/2010/06/10/2788.

Raish, C., W. Yong, and J. Marzluff. 1997. Contemporary human use of southwestern ponderosa pine forests. *In Songbird Ecology in Southwestern Ponderosa Pine Forests: A Literature Review.* USDA Forest Service General Technical Report RM-GTR-292, tech. eds. W. M. Block and D. M. Finch. 14 pp.

Stem decays and stains. In *Field Guide to Insects and Diseases of Arizona and New Mexico Forests.* http://www.fs.fed.us/r3/resources/health/field-guide/sds/bluestain.shtml.

Swetnam, T. W. 1984. Peeled ponderosa pine trees: A record of inner bark utilization by Native Americans. *Journal of Ethnobiology* 4 (2): 177–90.

Williams, G. W., comp. 2001. References on the American Indian use of fire in ecosystems. USDA Forest Service. http://www.wildlandfire.com/docs/biblio_indianfire.htm.

Wildflower Guides for the Southwest

Darrow, K. 2006. *Wild about Wildflowers*. Glendale, AZ: Wildcat Publishing Company. 224 pp.

Spellenberg, R. 1979. *The Audubon Society Field Guide to North American Wildflowers. Western Region.* New York: Alfred A. Knopf. 864 pp.

Index

Page numbers in **bold** indicate a diagram, figure, or photograph.

About the Author

Dr. Sylvester Allred taught more than twenty thousand students during his twenty-seven years as a biology professor at Northern Arizona University while also conducting research on the ecology and reproductive biology of tassel-eared squirrels within the ponderosa pine forests of the southwestern United States. He is the author of five children's books and *The Natural History of Tassel-Eared Squirrels*. One of his children's books, *Rascal, the Tassel-Eared Squirrel*, is about the first year of life of a tassel-eared squirrel living in the ponderosa pine forests at the Grand Canyon. He and his wife, Donna, moved to Durango, Colorado, in September 2012.